RED TEAMS AND COUNTERTERRORISM TRAINING

Red Teams and Counterterrorism Training

Stephen Sloan and
Robert J. Bunker

With a chapter
by Roberta Sloan

Foreword by David L. Boren

University of Oklahoma Press : Norman

Also by Stephen Sloan
Corporate Aviation Security: The Next Frontier in Aerospace Operations (coauthor)
Historical Dictionary of Terrorism (coauthor)
Low-Intensity Conflict: Old Threats in a New World (coeditor)
The Pocket Guide to Safe Travel
Responding to the Terrorist Threat: Security and Crisis Management (coeditor)
Simulating Terrorism
A Study in Political Violence: The Indonesian Experience
Terrorism: The Present Threat in Context

Also by Robert J. Bunker
Five-Dimensional (Cyber) Warfighting
Non-State Threats and Future Wars (editor)
Networks, Terrorism and Global Insurgency (editor)
Criminal-States and Criminal-Soldiers (editor)
Narcos over the Border: Gangs, Cartels and Mercenaries (editor)

Library of Congress Cataloging-in-Publication Data

Sloan, Stephen, 1936–
    Red teams and counterterrorism training / Stephen Sloan and Robert J. Bunker ; with a chapter by Roberta Sloan ; foreword by David L. Boren.
        p. cm.
    Includes bibliographical references and index.
    ISBN 978-0-8061-4183-1 (pbk. : alk. paper)
    1. Terrorism—Prevention. 2. Terrorism—Simulation methods. I. Bunker, Robert J. II. Title.
    HV6431.S559 2011
    363.325'160683—dc22

                                                    2010042823

In memory of Harriet Phillips, Frank Colavita,
and William Green

CONTENTS

ILLUSTRATIONS

FOREWORD

In this book Professor Stephen Sloan and Robert J. Bunker have given us a rare combination of theory and practical experience. Especially in the rapidly changing world of counterterrorism, the two perspectives are seldom combined with such a productive result.

Before it was fashionable, Sloan was thinking deeply about, examining, and writing about terrorism. I first met him when I left the U.S. Senate after chairing the Senate Select Committee on Intelligence for six years to become President of the University of Oklahoma. Because of our shared interest in intelligence issues, we sought out each other for conversations. I never left any of those conversations without having my assumptions challenged. There is nothing more important in the world of intelligence than continuing to think of all the possible outcomes and not just of the ones that have become accepted dogma.

Red Teams and Counterterrorism Training brings together the expertise of Sloan and Bunker in simulations and red teaming. It is based upon an understanding of terrorist behaviors that is acquired through years of study.

Bunker, an internationally recognized expert on non-state and unconventional threats to the United States, is, like Sloan, well versed in the topic. The author and editor of several books on terrorism, he bridges academic and professional realms as chief executive officer of Counter-OPFOR Corporation, a consulting firm that focuses on strategies to mitigate and respond to threats posed by non-state entities. Bunker has coordinated red team exercises for threat simulations ranging from an active shooter at a public school to a biological attack on a major subway system.

The concept of immersion to enable the red team to better understand the outlook of the adversary is effectively developed in a chapter by Roberta Sloan, Stephen's wife. She holds a doctorate in theater and has great insight into role-playing. To plan effectively, it is important to fully understand the feelings as well as the thoughts of terrorists.

Stephen Sloan continues to speak with great foresight. He has often said, "All terrorism is local." This insight became the basis for a national program to teach police officers how to recognize terrorism precursors. Stephen Sloan is a gifted teacher and he reveals his gift in this book.

Together, the Sloans and Bunker offer valuable tools that are essential for training responders for today's unique threats.

David L. Boren
Longest Serving Chair of the U.S. Senate
Select Committee on Intelligence
President of the University of Oklahoma

PREFACE

The simulation technique has proven invaluable in training those who fight terrorism. The origins and evolution of the simulation technique to provide the most realistic and useful training for those individuals, organizations, and units responsible for countering terrorism resulted from many different factors. Taken individually, these factors may have been unrelated, but as a totality, they provided an integrated approach to combat what is now recognized as a major threat to global, national, and personal security. In a very real sense, the first version of this book *(Simulating Terrorism)* was the product of a combination of intellectual interests forged and shaped by the hammer of experience. This is even more true of the vastly revised *Red Teams and Counterterrorism Training,* a collaboration between both the original author, Stephen Sloan, and the coauthor of the current volume, Robert J. Bunker.

STEPHEN SLOAN

My intellectual interest started in high school when a wonderful social studies teacher introduced me to the world of history and politics. That interest was refined during my studies as a political science major in college and especially as a graduate student majoring in Southeast Asian area studies and comparative government in the late 1950s and the '60s. During those decades, the great optimism that the end of colonial rule would lead to prosperity and development in what was then called the Third World was increasingly tempered by the violence that went along with wars of national liberation—the communal strife, insurgency and counterinsurgency, and other forms of armed conflict and political violence that accompanied the idealized transition "from empire to nation."[1] The role of violence took on even greater meaning for this would-be Southeast Asian specialist when I took a course on Vietnamese politics in 1962, before the conflict in Indochina surfaced as the cause of a defining and turbulent time on the American landscape.

As a result of my studies, I decided to conduct my field research in Indonesia. This country, under the leadership of President Sukarno, had vied to be a leader of the new states of Asia and Africa since the Bandung Conference of 1955. Indonesia, with its massive population, great diversity, and successful armed conflict against the Dutch, represented both the hopes and the concerns of those who wished that independence would resolve the many problems the new governments faced. As a result, in 1965 I went to Jakarta to study student indoctrination programs that ideally sought to establish a sense of national identity among the different ethnic, tribal, and religious groups in the archipelago but were in many ways the arena in which competing political forces—nationalists, communists, religious parties, and the military—sought to establish their respective views on the minds of a postcolonial generation.

This political competition would be transformed into a major physical upheaval when on the evening of September 30, 1965, there was an attempted coup, ostensibly led by the Communist Party of Indonesia (PKI). The full facts of the coup attempt are still heatedly debated and will not be addressed here.[2] I witnessed the physical conflict in Jakarta at this time, as the army sought to avenge the death of its generals and establish control and Islamic opponents of the PKI called for jihad against the party, which they characterized as being anti-Islamic and "Satans of the city and countryside." The voice and actions of fundamentalism were heard long before the current concerns over global jihadists.

A visit to Bali a few weeks after the coup attempt brought home the reality of violence as I witnessed the burning of villages of individuals who were accused of being communists—more often than not, wrongly. What was especially frightening was that the violence that took place often had no relationship to politics but was primal in nature: a means to settle old scores, blood feuds, and any other real or imagined insults. For example, one peasant, when asked whether the people of the burning villages were involved in the coup, chillingly replied, "The people in the other village are devils."[3] In the ensuing months, those primal feelings, often justified by politics, would lead to the death of over half a million people. My introduction to this violence was thus a transformational experience in which I was unwillingly forced to recognize the centrality of violence in political life.[4]

Upon my return home, I was offered several positions in Southeast Asia related to the growing involvement of the United States in Vietnam. The offers were financially attractive and, for a young man, adventurous. They involved, among other things, plotting potential maritime infiltration of the U.S. Navy through junk identification aboard a Thai-crewed ship in the Gulf of Tonkin. A second opportunity took the form of attitude surveys related to a growing insurgency in northeastern Thailand. I decided not to take up the offers, because I wanted to complete my dissertation and recognized that, if I went overseas, the likelihood of my returning to an academic career—I had at this point taught for two years in a liberal arts college—would be questionable. But the Indonesian experience developed within me not only a lifelong commitment to study violence but also a need to combine this academic interest with a desire to return to the field and be involved in understanding and addressing violence and conflict.

It was at the University of Oklahoma, over a span of thirty-eight years, that I was able to combine my academic and operational interests. The university had a pioneering program in public administration that sent faculty all over the world to various military installations and locations. In this program, I began to discuss and work with those individuals and groups who were on the forefront of countering insurgencies as part of their professional duties. For example, students would fly to Guam or Okinawa to take my class on transitional politics or insurgency and then return "in country." This tradition continued until my retirement, although in later years, my students were returning from or going on their first, second, or third tours of duty in Iraq and Afghanistan. My dedication to strengthening the nexus between academia and the so-called "real world" was thereby enhanced over time.

In the mid-1970s, I made a fundamental transition: while political violence, armed conflict, and insurgency remained major areas of interest, I began to focus on terrorism. Indeed, my first graduate class on international terrorism may have been the first one given in the United States and probably the first listed as such in a college catalogue.

The primary impetus for this change resulted from my first visit to Israel in 1974. Despite the incidents of terrorism in Europe and the Middle East, particularly the Munich Massacre, I was struck upon my return that there was virtually no academic writing on contemporary terrorists and, with the exception of efforts of such pioneers as Brian Jenkins of the RAND Corporation, there were no centers in or outside of academia that focused on terrorism. Especially within political science, the study of terrorism, when it did exist, was done by scholars who were often isolated, because terrorism was not recognized as a legitimate topic for study. While there has been considerable improvement, terrorism studies still are not yet within the mainstream of political science.[5]

Without the outstanding students I had in my first seminars on terrorism, I might not have pursued the development of this new field. Their contributions to initial research included comparative analysis of incidents in the absence of databases, much less a larger body of knowledge on terrorism. In addition, many of the students experienced a unique "final examination" when they took on the roles of hostages, terrorists, and members of the media in end-of-course simulations in the United States and overseas.[6] Members of my informal study group on international terrorism and those who followed not only have continued in the field but also are now leading authorities or senior officials in the counterterrorism community.

Concomitantly, a major change in the budding research agenda took place as the result of the work Dr. Roberta Raider Sloan, my wife, who is Professor of Theater at Temple University. From her time as a graduate student to the present, she has had a long-term commitment to teaching the techniques of and performing in improvisational theater. Interested in moving beyond traditional publication in peer-reviewed journals, I wondered how to apply these early research findings to address the challenges created by threats and incidents of terrorism. With Roberta's insights, I realized that using the techniques of improvisational theater in highly realistic exercises would be useful in training and challenging organizations that wanted to not only effectively respond to but also take the initiative away from the terrorists. This fusion of intellectual interests, academic specialization, and experience along with a desire to move beyond the confines of the university campus continues today.

ROBERT J. BUNKER

While the circumstances leading up to Stephen Sloan's concern with terrorism were largely birthed in the turbulence of the 1960s, my commitment to addressing the problem came later, after the concept was entrenched in the nation's psyche. My intellectual interest in war, conflict, and ultimately counterterrorism was (like Sloan's) cultivated at a young age. Raised by my father, a retired Marine lieutenant colonel who served in World War II and Korea, I developed an early interest in military affairs. A youthful desire to put what I read in military manuals and the *Marine Corps Gazette* into practice led to a serious interest in war gaming and simulations. Television images of the injustices inflicted upon the United States with the final evacuation from Saigon in 1975, the Iran hostage crisis in 1979–81, and the 1983 Beirut barracks bombing during my teen and early adult years solidified my steadfast opposition to insurgents and terrorists.

My multiple college majors (in history, anthropology-geography, social science, and behavioral science) provided a broad education on the interaction of factors related to major historical change. This understanding was further filled out through numerous military science courses offered by the campus Army ROTC. Most of my research focused on military history, war, and conflict. The discovery of RAND reports in the library stacks led me to the works of Brian Jenkins. Jenkins's eye-opening *New Modes of Conflict* (then a new work) discussed a future that would see the blending of conventional war, guerilla war, and terrorism—elements of what today many term "hybrid war."[7]

My time in graduate school culminated in a master's degree in government and a doctorate in political science. Given the full support of my faculty advisor and another mentor, I tailored my research toward terrorists and guerillas, biological and chemical warfare, classical warfare, and strategic simulation and modeling. My dissertation work focused on exploring patterns of medieval and modern warfare, the effects of catastrophic military defeat, and political change centered on the state of Brandenburg-Prussia. Years of doctoral research resulted in a body of original theoretical work termed Fourth Epoch War theory that foresaw the rise of nonstate entities emerging to threaten the national security interests of the

United States. Having prepared for over a decade for some sort of "firebreak" to be crossed and the wars with the nonstate entities to be openly declared, I was not surprised by the occurrence of an event on the level of 9/11.[8]

Unlike Dr. Sloan, who has both benefited from and, at times, felt isolated by his academic peers for being a tenured professor with expertise in counterterrorism, my professional work experience since the early 1990s has shifted between academia and research, consulting and contracting, and quasi-official positions of public service and trust. While this makes me something of an anomaly among mainstream political science academics, the upside is that it has provided a unique perspective concerning different facets of how the counterterrorism world operates. Some of my past positions have included national security studies, political science, and military history teaching as an adjunct professor at California State University–San Bernardino (1994–2002); being a counterterrorism and less-lethal-weapons consultant to the National Law Enforcement and Corrections Technology Center–West (NLECTC–West, 2000–2007); and being the futurist in residence with the Behavioral Science Unit, FBI Academy (2006–2007). I was also one of the last two original members still with the Los Angeles Terrorism Early Warning Group (LA TEW, beginning in 1996 and ending in 2009). My current positions are that of CEO of the Counter-OPFOR Corporation (beginning in 2005) and recently that of an adjunct instructor, teaching homeland security and public policy, at the University of Southern California.

From a terrorism red teaming and simulation perspective, a close association with the LA TEW, and later NLECTC–West, enabled me to construct the needed bridge between counterterrorism theory (academic thinking) and application (law enforcement operations). The years right after 9/11 accelerated this process as I left the world of university teaching and took on what an associate would term a "combat support role" to Los Angeles and western states' law enforcement agencies that were faced with the specter of further terrorist attacks. My "gray area" status between being a ordinary citizen (noncombatant) and a responder (law enforcement officer or combatant) provided me with many opportunities to engage in training in terrorism-related disciplines, including kidnapping, assassination, facility seizure, assault weapons and improvised explosive devices (IEDs), countersurveillance, hazardous materials (HAZMAT) response, intelligence techniques, and even simulated mock IED emplacements in crowded public facilities. My intent has been to become not a responder but a better counterterrorism applied theorist, educator and trainer, and operational support team member.

My recent exercise coordination and trainer experience includes being red team coordinator for a simulated biological attack in 2005 on a major metropolitan subway system, an active shooter trainer in 2007 for law enforcement response at a public high school, and the red team coordinator in 2008 for a simulated suicide-bomber radiological attack on a nationally televised parade. The creation of an annotated FBI Library subject bibliography titled *Red Teaming* in late 2008 and being on the *Red Team Journal* advisory board have assisted in keeping me current in this discipline. In addition, I have produced over 150 publications, including scholarly works such as edited books and peer-reviewed journal articles, tactical-level publications for special weapons and tactics (SWAT) personnel, and suicide bomber and laser devices (and weapons) response guidance for law enforcement.[9] One of these publications (on the topic of street gangs evolving into paramilitary groups, which came out in 1996 in a law enforcement journal) elicited a warm letter from Dr. Sloan, thus beginning our many years of professional association.[10]

THE COLLABORATION

First and foremost, this work is intended for applied use by U.S. police agencies—local, state, and federal—with a secondary audience in the military services. This work may also find its way into certain university-level courses on counterterrorism and homeland security. Those in the general public who wish to have a better understanding of a threat that they and their family and friends cannot afford to dismiss (or overreact to) will also benefit from this book.[11] We hope that these latter readers will be inspired by some of the concepts and hard-won lessons learned in the text and someday stand shoulder-to-shoulder with the rest of us in defense of country against the scourges of terrorism that, unfortunately, shows no signs of abating in the early years of the twenty-first century.

ORGANIZATION OF THE BOOK

Why should we have a course on terrorism? It does not fit
into the mainstream of the discipline or our curriculum.
—Political science professor, 1975

Red Teams and Counterterrorism Training comprises eight chapters, three appendixes, and a selected bibliography. We have
made a concerted effort to avoid jargon and academic verbiage
throughout the book. However, because acronyms are commonly used at both tactical and operational levels of response
within the counterterrorism discipline, a glossary listing these
acronyms and other specialized terminology is provided.

Chapter 1, "Terrorism and Simulations Today," addresses
how assumptions that guided the planning and conduct of the
simulations described in the original edition of this book have
been modified over the years because of the transformation of
the terrorist threat landscape. These changes relate both to behavioral factors and to such technological developments as the
creation of the Internet, as well as increasingly profound altera-
tions in the international system ranging from the emergence
of nonstate actors to the impact of globalization. The general
requirements for modifying and refining the original simulation technique to adjust to the changes are discussed.

Chapter 2, "Basic Principles of Conducting a Simulation,"
provides an essential overview of the basic principles that
should guide the development, conduct, and evaluation of
simulations. The basic principles are generic and can (and

should) be modified to meet the unique requirements of each simulation.

Chapter 3, "Guiding the Simulation," focuses on the administrative and organizational prerequisites to successfully conduct a simulation. Such basic issues as the need to reconcile safety with realism and the vital need for command support are presented.

Chapter 4, "Murphy's Law Can Prove Fatal," updates the type of miscalculations that can take place in a simulation and suggests how "lessons learned" can help to prevent mistakes that could prove fatal in an actual incident. The "lessons learned" cited in this chapter are based in part on the simulations conducted by Bunker and Sloan as well as on crucial case studies.

Chapter 5, "The Red Team: Developing an Adversarial Perspective," largely draws on Bunker's simulation experience in systematically addressing the issues and requirements pertaining to the use of red teams and why different OPFOR (opposing force) levels of sophistication must be considered when conducting simulations.

Chapter 6, "Getting the Red Team Ready for Its Role," is a contribution written by Dr. Roberta Sloan. It focuses on theater and improvisation techniques that will allow red team members to more convincingly get into their roles, enhancing the simulation experience for the police and counterterrorism forces undergoing the training.

Chapter 7, "Terrorist Attack Cycle," elaborates on the planning, preparation, and execution phases of the terrorist attack cycle. The chapter draws on William McRaven's concepts of relative superiority and John Boyd's OODA (observe, orient, decide, act) loops and their relationship to the terrorist attack cycle. The intent of this chapter is to enable those involved in counterterrorism to better understand the tactics and operations of sophisticated terrorists as well as lesser threats such as amateur terrorists and teenage active shooters.

Chapter 8, "Future Terrorism: Out-Innovating the Terrorists," assesses future trends in terrorist tactics and strategies to make the case for the development of simulations that can seize the initiative from the terrorists. In addition to early warning considerations, a futures perspective is taken in this chapter; this will provide responders with innovative opportunities to be capitalized upon. Topics covered include terrorist use of exotic and directed energy weaponry, dual-dimensional and cyberspace operations, and network organizational forms, along with private security forces and mercenaries and long-term community disruption potentials.

The first two appendixes provide generic simulation guidance that can be modified to meet the requirement of terrorist simulations based on the threat environment and missions of the counterterrorism organizations and forces involved in the simulations. The final appendix discusses the need for actionable intelligence within the context of the active-aggressor incident that recently took place in Fort Hood, Texas.

Appendix 1, "Intelligence-Driven Simulations," focuses on the means to conduct exercises that test the ability of authorities to collect, analyze, and act through the effective use of counterterrorism intelligence. This capability is important not only for the particular challenges created by threats of weapons of mass destruction but also for more common threats such as active shooters, active assaults, and suicide bomber operations.

Appendix 2, "Hostage-Taking and Active-Aggressor Simulations," concerns the dynamics inherent in determining what type of emergency situation is taking place—one in which hostages are being taken versus one in which individuals are immediately being killed. The appropriate identification of the incident will drive the initial response to it, based on either talking (negotiation) or shooting (tactical assault). Combined-approach considerations are also touched upon, along with major simulation requirements.

Appendix 3, "The Cost of Failures in Intelligence: The Tragedy of Fort Hood," helps to highlight the simulation guidance provided in the first two appendixes, providing a short discussion illustrative of the critical need for actionable intelligence. Such intelligence failed to be developed in the Fort Hood incident because specific links were not made between the prevailing strategic intelligence that existed and the intelligence that was generated prior to the incident.

The bibliography primarily incorporates key books and articles pertaining to the simulation of terrorism, its relationship to red teams, and counterterrorism operations. The intent is to provide readers with the ability to further educate themselves in this arena and gain the necessary background and confidence needed to then professionally reach out to others in the counterterrorism community.

The following chapters draw on some of the material and themes from *Simulating Terrorism*, but extensive revisions were made—for all intents and purposes, this is a new work and not merely a new edition—to take into account the continuity and change that have accompanied the evolution of terrorism since the publication of the previous book in 1981. Many changes reflect the continuing refinement of the simulation techniques based on experience, including exercises conducted by Stephen Sloan after his initial book was published and also the more recent work of Robert Bunker as he engaged in cutting-edge contemporary simulation techniques. Moreover, necessary modifications to the simulations are assessed in terms of their ability to meet contemporary and future developments in understanding the motivations, intentions, capabilities, tactics, and strategies of terrorists and other violent nonstate actors. In addition to changes that take into account the influence of individual and organizational behavior, technological developments that can be used by or against terrorists also have a profound impact on the dynamics of adjusting simulations to meet the transforming threat environment. Modifications in the simulation techniques thus are not necessarily reactive in nature but permit counterterrorism units to take the initiative and the offensive in not only anticipating future terrorism developments but also out-innovating the terrorists.

For too long, authorities at all levels have largely found themselves in a posture of reaction or, even worse, damage control with regard to the physical, political, economic, social, and organizational costs after an act or campaign of terrorism. The refined techniques discussed in this book therefore also focus on developing the necessary simulations to enable authorities both to prevent acts from occurring and to address where terrorism preemption fits in, that is, seizing the initiative from adversaries (often very determined) who are engaging in a form of protracted warfare. Finally, the revisions of the simulation technique address hard issues of policies and the means to test them in order to provide guidance and leadership for effective operations against terrorists. Such guidance must go beyond the requirement of educating those directly involved in countering terrorism: there is a great need for educating the public in regard to dealing with threats and acts of terrorism.

Abbreviations

AOG	Army of God
APC	armored personnel carrier
ATD	advanced technology demonstration
ATF	Bureau of Alcohol, Tobacco, Firearms, and Explosives
Cal/OSHA	California Division of Occupational Safety and Health
CBRN	chemical, biological, radiological, and nuclear
CBRNE	chemical, biological, radiological, nuclear, and (high yield) explosives
C/E	controller and evaluator
CERT	community emergency response team
CNN	Cable News Network
CST	civil support team
DEA	Drug Enforcement Agency
DHS	Department of Homeland Security
EEG	exercise evaluation guide
ExPlan	exercise plan
FAO	foreign area officer
FBI	Federal Bureau of Investigation
FLETC	Federal Law Enforcement Training Center

FWG	Futures Working Group
GPS	Global Positioning System
GSG 9	Grenzschutzgruppe 9
HAZMAT	hazardous material
HSEEP	Homeland Security Exercise and Evaluation Program
HUMINT	human intelligence
ICS	incident command system
IED	improvised explosive device
IPO	intelligence preparation for operations
IRA	Irish Republican Army
I&W	indications and warnings
JTTF	joint terrorism task force
MANPADS	man-portable air defense systems
MOOSEMUSS	maneuver, objective, offense, simplicity, economy of force, mass, unity of command, surprise, and security
MSEL	master scenario events list
NIMS	National Incident Management System
NLECTC	National Law Enforcement and Corrections Technology Center
NTOA	National Tactical Officers Association
OODA	observe, orient, decide, and act
OIC	officer in charge
OPFOR	opposing force
OPSEC	operational security
Optempo	operational tempo
OSHA	Occupational Safety and Health Administration
O-SMEAC	orientation, situation, mission, execution, administration/logistics, and command/signal
PFLP	Popular Front for the Liberation of Palestine
PIO	public information officer
PKI	Communist Party of Indonesia

RAF	Red Army Faction
ROTC	Reserve Officers Training Corps
RPG	rocket-propelled grenade
SAS	Special Air Services
SASO	stability and support operations
SitMan	situation manual
SOF	Special Operations Forces
Spec Ops	special operations
STRATCOM	Strategic Command
SWAT	special weapons and tactics
TAC	terrorist attack cycle
TEW	terrorism early warning group
TLO	terrorism liaison officer
TRC	Terrorism Research Center
UFMCS	University of Foreign Military and Cultural Studies
VBIED	vehicular-borne improvised explosive device
VCC	Virtual Command Center
VIP	very important person
WMD	weapons of mass destruction
ZOG	Zionist Occupation Government

Red Teams and Counterterrorism Training

CHAPTER 1

TERRORISM AND SIMULATIONS TODAY

Their drills were bloodless battles, and their battles were bloody drills.

—Josephus's commentary on the Roman army

When *Simulating Terrorism* was published, its author, Stephen Sloan, was literally navigating in an uncharted intellectual and operational environment. Sloan based the development of the simulations therein on the tactics and strategies of the terrorists in the mid-1970s and early '80s. Part of the analysis underlying these simulations was based on groundbreaking research, at a time when there were relatively few systematic examinations of terrorist acts and campaigns of terrorism.[1] Part was also based on the findings of the study group on international terrorism that was established in 1976—findings that would be published in various works in the ensuing years.[2] The simulations were based on the author's changing research agenda and interests that reflected his assessment of changes in the terrorist landscape.

Starting in 1976, Sloan conducted full simulations ranging from the first terrorism-related exercise with the University of Oklahoma Police Department at their shooting range to the "seizure" of a major refinery in Tulsa, Oklahoma, where the Tulsa Police were confronted with a "well trained and highly armed group" that threatened to blow up the facility if their demands were not met. Additional exercises followed, including one with the New Zealand Police in conjunction with their hostage negotiation course, the simulated seizure of police officers at Portland International Airport, and a test of base security with units of the Fifty-first Security Police Squadron at Osan Airbase, Korea. With the completion of the book, these exercises continued, including a simulation lasting for more than twenty-four hours that matched the Berlin Brigade against (unknown to Sloan at the time) what was then a secret U.S. Delta Force detachment posted to Berlin. In all these simulations and those that followed, Sloan was fortunate to work with leadership and organizations willing to test their abilities against a threat that still appeared remote to most Americans, who viewed acts of terrorism as tragic occurrences that happened to other people in other countries.

As a result, both those involved in conducting the simulations and those who responded to them were engaging in pioneering work to meet a threat that remained below the radar to political leaders and policy makers, especially in the United States. While it may now be difficult to believe, one had to "sell" the terrorist threat to organizations that felt that they had more pressing demands and could not afford "the luxury" of addressing what Brian Jenkins had presciently called "a new mode of conflict."[3] Even internationally, despite what could be called the beginning of modern terrorism—the Munich Massacre of 1972 and the hostage takings and bombings that took place, especially in the United Kingdom, Western Europe, and the Middle East—security authorities and civilian and uniformed forces were only just beginning to refine their counterterrorism capabilities. When there were simulations, they were often done in secret and very selectively for such elite units as the then West German GSG 9, the U.S. Delta Force, and the British SAS. The technique of developing and conducting full-scale simulations was still an evolving and very uncertain art.

DEVELOPING SIMULATION TECHNIQUES

The inertia that characterized counterterrorism training, especially in the United States, had started to change after the aborted attempted rescue of the hostages in Iran in 1976. But domestically, the development of simulations as a technique to respond to the terrorist threat would not be fully recognized even with the first bombing of the World Trade Center in 1993. It would take the profound shocks created by the destruction of the Federal Building in Oklahoma City in 1995 and the events of 9/11 to finally energize the political leadership, police, and military forces to develop and conduct full-scale simulations. As often happens when spurred by crises, Washington went from a posture of underreaction in terms of conducting exercises to perceivably one of overreaction, as illustrated by the activities of the Homeland Security Department in such simulations as "Top Off" and similar ones that followed. These exercises, however, took place after the fact and often adhered to the manner of addressing a challenge by "throwing money at the problem." Moreover, the large size and complexity of these later simulations can be an impediment for learning to combat those who have engaged in massive destruction and the generation of fear by adhering to the principle that "small is beautiful"—and also lethal. We now face determined adversaries who have often brilliantly engaged in "asymmetric warfare," whereby the strength of a far more powerful opponent is turned into vulnerability. Those who practice contemporary terrorism have learned this lesson well.[4]

Greeted with indifference when he embarked on the study of terrorism in the 1970s, Sloan finds it vexing when he is told (as often occurs) that he has selected a "hot topic." It is both ironic and tragic that the topic is "hot" and will unfortunately become "hotter" as a new generation of terrorists refines the tactics and strategies employed against governments that are, in too many cases, still primarily reactive after an incident occurs. The fact that terrorist simulations have become "respectable" (indeed, part of the conventional wisdom in dealing with such threats and acts) makes it even more important to revisit the breakthroughs of Sloan's original work, *Simulating Terrorism*, and address both the continuity and the change inherent in modern terrorism.

REVISING EARLY ASSUMPTIONS AND INCORPORATING NEW ONES

Although bombing was the major mode of terrorist operations during the 1970s (as it is now), there was particular concern over how to deal with hostage taking. The seizure of the Israeli athletes in 1972, hostage taking by such groups as the Red Army Faction (RAF) in Germany and the Red Brigades in Italy, and the continuing seizure of aircraft by the Popular Front for the Liberation of Palestine (PFLP) and others forced governments not only to address the need to develop hostage negotiation techniques but also to acquire the operational abilities to engage in what was often called "siege management." In addition, law enforcement both in the United States and in Western Europe was addressing the challenge of hostage taking in terms of "barricade-hostage" situations.

Ironically, the latter was in part the result of an improvement in law enforcement response to incidents. Because of the development and use of silent alarms, television cameras, and other communication technologies in banks and stores, the police would often arrive during an incident instead of after it. While one response to these developments was the creation and training of special weapons and tactics teams (SWAT), there was a growing awareness that such teams could not be a substitute for skilled hostage negotiators. These negotiators had acquired the necessary techniques in such countries as the United Kingdom and the Netherlands in response to high-profile incidents as well as in the pioneering units in the United States, most notably those of the New York Police Department.[5]

Sloan's research agenda well matched this concern, since the study group findings addressed the interaction between terrorists and authorities during a hostage situation, in contrast to a bombing, in which case there was no negotiation and the response took place after the casualties and physical damage had already been done. The simulations, therefore, sought to focus on and replicate an ongoing process in which the police or military would have to address the options for both negotiation and force as part of their training requirements in dealing with politically motivated terrorist attacks and hostage situations ranging from abortive bank robberies to domestic disputes.

Assumptions

Some of the assumptions that guided the early development of these simulations may still be valid, while others have not weathered the test of time. The latter must be modified to meet current conditions in order for this technique to continue to anticipate future terrorists' motivations and capabilities as well as to evaluate the vulnerability of human and physical targets. Many terrorist groups today proclaim their commitment to supplant contemporary political and social orders with idealized traditional ones (often based on a particular interpretation of a religion). In a most profound manner, while the impact of globalization has led to greater interdependence among people, it has also resulted in a call for a reassertion of traditional values against those of modernity and secular mass society. Even as they look backward for inspiration, however, these groups have increasingly been innovative in their use of technology. Moreover, with the end of the cold war, a wide variety of new players have emerged to play their respective role in international politics. The changing terrorist threat environment does not mean that traditional tactics of terrorism will not continue. Bombings, the use of handheld weapons, hostage taking, and the panoply of tried-and-true assaults on civil order remain in use. Ultimately, however, there have been enough significant changes in terrorist values and capabilities to necessitate concurrent changes in assumptions in order to effectively simulate our present realities and those of the foreseeable future. The following assumptions of the original work no longer hold up in today's threat environment.

Force should only be used as a last resort. The development of the original simulations was based on assumptions derived from comparative analysis of incidents of terrorism and the operational requirement to deal with them. In the early studies on the tactical response, over 79 percent of the casualties took place when an incident was resolved by the use of force.[6] Therefore, in the event of a terrorist incident involving the taking of hostages, the use of force was considered a last resort; a tactical response—however sophisticated—was perceived as being on the razor's edge of failure and could lead to the injuring or death of the hostages and members of the responding forces.

Earlier patterns of terrorism have now changed, and responding forces are being faced with incidents in which executions and the killing of innocents begin immediately. Increasingly, there are those who, because of their beliefs, are not concerned about public opinion as in the past, and they are willing to immediately kill hostages. They have no desire to negotiate, because their expected rewards are not based on achieving goals in this life but are instead granted in the next. The problem is further exacerbated by the increase in the number and frequency of "school shootings." These cases involve "active shooters," requiring law enforcement to take immediate action with ad hoc responding forces to save lives. As a result, modern standard operating procedures should dictate that the use of force not be considered only as a last resort.

Time is on the side of the authorities. This earlier perception derived from the prevailing counterterrorism dictum driving the emphasis on negotiations. Because time was said to be on the side of the authorities, the following assumptions were considered valid: (a) while the hostage-takers might control the area where they held the hostages, beyond that the authorities had the advantage; (b) as a result, the hostage-takers in a protracted incident would be in need of food, electricity, cigarettes, and other goods and services for both the perpetrators and the hostages. This could allow the negotiation process to offer a tangible quid pro quo such as the exchange of hostages for commodities. There was more than one incident, for example, in which a heavy smoker would give up a hostage for a cigarette if he had additional captives.

Moreover, there was recognition with regard to hostage taking that the "Stockholm Syndrome" could work in two ways to affect the outcome of a negotiation process. In the case of that notable robbery in Stockholm, several of the hostages identified with their captor and, among other things, were unwilling to testify against him at the trial. Conversely, the hostage taker might identify with his captives, therefore humanizing them and becoming reluctant to use violence against them.[7] When the initial simulations took place, police were only beginning to engage in hostage negotiation training, and as noted earlier, the exercises both addressed and furthered the training. The outcome of these programs over the following years was indeed impressive; in captivities not resulting from acts of terrorism, a skilled negotiation team has made all the difference. That such a team could also make a difference where terrorists were involved was postulated.

This pattern of terrorism, however, has to a marked degree changed; with the heightened levels of violence now taking place, many incidents resemble mini-military engagements, with victory going to the side having faster operational capabilities. Therefore, the view should be taken that time is not always on the side of the authorities in negotiating because:

(a) you have a state that either directly or indirectly supports those who are engaging in a hostage taking; (b) you have a "failed state," which lacks the capability to counter the terrorists; (c) you have terrorists as nonstate actors who deny and therefore ignore the legitimacy of a state to negotiate with them; or (d) you cannot hope for a reverse "Stockholm Syndrome," either because immediate and often fatal violence has been perpetrated against hostages or because the captor has already dehumanized his captives on ethnic, racial, religious, or other grounds and views them as little more than animals.

An immediate defensive or reactive response to a terrorism incident is sufficient. When the initial simulations were planned and executed, they primarily dealt with response to incidents, since that was the major concern of the police and military forces. In a very real sense, this posture was a manifestation of the fact that, in the early days of dealing with terrorism, countries and their forces were on the defensive against actions by armed adversaries that they had not anticipated or understood. It was a slow and painful learning curve. As a result, in preparing for simulations, relatively little attention was directed at providing the scenarios and training for the pre-incident phases involved in a terrorist act (for example, organizing and recruiting terrorists, initial target selection, or surveillance) prior to "going tactical" (that is, moving to the target and initiating the attack).

With regard to law enforcement, this reactive mode was part of an orientation that placed little emphasis on the intelligence function. Police intelligence, where it existed, was limited and primarily tactical in nature. As a result, these forces, especially on the state and local level, understandably lacked the capacity to engage in an effective intelligence process, much less deal with the unique complexities of what would become the requirement for counterterrorism intelligence. The military was clearly more equipped to deal with the challenge, but their targets of intelligence were primarily conventional forces, and the analysis of terrorist threats, where it existed, was largely focused on the threat of insurgencies. Moreover, the military police, like the U.S. armed services at large, did not view terrorism as a strategic threat but relegated it essentially to crime and therefore considered that it fell under the auspices of law enforcement. Hence, starting in the 1970s, whether one looked at civilian or military forces, counterterrorism intelligence as a field had not been initiated, much less refined.

Over the ensuing years, Sloan increasingly tested the counterterrorism intelligence process. He shares the view held by Bunker, among others, that the first defense against terrorism is good intelligence and, accordingly, acknowledges the necessity of collecting information, analyzing terrorist activities, and disseminating the product in the form of actionable intelligence to all necessary parties—from state and local to national and international levels.[8] By testing and refining the intelligence process in simulations, one can better evaluate the potential for incidents in the pre-incident phase and ideally apprehend the terrorists before they "go tactical." This change is especially needed now, given the availability of WMD, for, if these weapons are used, the magnitude of the damage will move beyond crisis or emergency management to damage control and physical and organizational triage. A defensive response is not sufficient, and the prevention or preemption of a terrorist incident should be made a priority. Even a failed terrorist attack can be considered a success from a disruptive targeting perspective; for that reason, counterterrorism intelligence-driven simulations now need to be conducted.

Relations between the police and the press are stable and the press will respect police wishes to avoid compromising an incident. This is a far different world from the one in which the initial exercises took place. In all those exercises, the relationship between the police and media was tested, though the press was at that time less confrontational in their desire to bolster ratings and viewership. The focus at that time was on both print and electronic media.[9] Police and press relations have now been made more complex as a result of the development of the Internet, the proliferation of television channels, struggles over viewer market share, and the existence of an alternative media universe with new players now gaining media capabilities. Today, news media outlets of the United States and its allies no longer always honor police wishes, due to the intense competition between them to get the latest "breaking news" story. This was vividly portrayed during the North Hollywood shootout in February 1997 and the immediate coverage of all ensuing tragedies and events of a sensational nature. Further, foreign media groups such as the Al Jazeera news network and specialized terrorist and insurgent media cells have created media entities that are specifically hostile to U.S. police and military agencies.

Of further concern is the "emergence of virtual terrorism . . . the ability and willingness of terrorists to alter and magnify their threat capabilities by altering the perception of the people watching through the use of the internet and other forms of communication."[10] Now the responders to a terrorist incident must concern themselves not only with the actions of the threat groups involved but also with those of the media and make a determination of their status as friends, neutrals, or hostile forces controlled by foreign entities or even the terrorists themselves.

Additional Guiding Principles

Unity of action. In revising the simulation technique, the authors recognize that, on the one hand, "all terrorism is local"— that is, at the inception of a threat or incident, the authorities in the immediate jurisdiction will probably be the first to respond to an act or campaign of terrorism. On the other hand, given the regional and international scope of terrorists' activities, it will be increasingly vital to train jurisdictions to develop unity of action instead of engaging in interdepartmental and interagency competition. Moreover, on the regional and international level, different governments must also achieve unity of action instead of having their own form of what can be called jurisdictional gridlock based on the impediments of sovereignty and disparate national security concerns and requirements. Terrorists have too often achieved the ability to ignore the arbitrary boundaries of nation-states, while national authorities still have not reduced the impediments preventing concerted action in what in the final analysis is an increasingly interdependent world. The refinement of simulations must help promote cooperation at all levels from the state and local to the regional and, ultimately, the international arena.

Getting into character. A pioneering effort was made in the original work to inculcate what is now called "the red team" into the simulations. These pioneers recognized that not only the tactical techniques of the terrorists should be used but also that the individuals who played such roles should be indoctrinated into the terrorists' values and beliefs and acquire a terrorist perspective in planning and conducting an operation. Terrorist role players were often required to write out their personal histories and ideological views to help get them into character. Ultimately, though, the focus was on training the responding forces and not emphasizing the creation of a "terrorist mindset," so red team development was still limited, and in some instances, red team members (specifically, U.S. military personnel) were not psychologically suited to their roles. Updated simulation techniques need to focus on the needs of red team creation and how to get red team members into their roles in order for that team to mirror the behavior, actions, and specific level of sophistication of a threat group for simulation purposes.

Opposing-force simulations are becoming more realistic, with a broader pool of active-aggressor role players including women and those from divergent ethnic backgrounds. In this photo, a member of opposing forces engages U.S. soldiers, airmen, and Marines with an M-16 rifle at Avon Park Air Ground Training Complex, Florida, June 16, 2008, during Atlantic Strike VII. Atlantic Strike is a semiannual joint forces training exercise involving the U.S. Army, U.S. Air Force, and U.S. Marine Corps assigned to joint terminal attack controllers. Courtesy of U.S. Air Force/photo by Staff Sgt. Stephen J. Otero (released).

Determining failure or success. Current simulations have become so complex that, as noted earlier, they do not effectively counter the organizational doctrine of terrorist groups. Too often these simulations have become heavily politicized as responding law enforcement agencies want to look good and thus are reluctant to have the flexible, unpredictable, and demanding training that is a must if they are truly to acquire the ability to counter dedicated terrorists. This has also become a major problem for high-profile military simulations. In extreme cases, the simulation scripts have been so crafted that the good guys will always win and that few to no casualties will take place. In other instances, candid hot washes, lessons learned, and after-action reports are either not conducted or not acted upon. Judging the failure or success of a given simulation may also be based on attendance at planning meetings, following proper budget accounting procedures, and compliance with mountains of paperwork and reports so that the bureaucrats and middle managers are appeased. The revised simulations should be kept at the operational and tactical levels with rank and politics kept out of them as much as possible. Mistakes should be expected as part of the learning process. These simulations need to address how existing organizations can, from the bottom up, develop the unity of purpose, the small size, and the flexibility to counter asymmetric adversaries.

CHAPTER 2

Basic Principles of Conducting a Simulation

Complexity is easy to attain; simplicity is difficult to achieve.

—Sloan's experience in dealing with
bureaucracy in conducting simulations

Whether one is planning a basic simulation for a small organization or one of its subunits or a complex multijurisdictional simulation, there are basic principles that should be considered in the preparation, conduct, and evaluation of the exercises. These generic principles should be adjusted to meet the unique requirements of those responsible for the simulation. The following principles are based on the experience of both authors in developing and participating in numerous exercises as well as present and longer-term changes in the terrorist threat environment that must be anticipated and prepared for.

SIMULATIONS GO BEYOND GAMING AND COMMAND POST EXERCISES

Simulations differ from gaming and command post exercises. The former essentially presents background material for the players, provides the basic rules of the exercise, and—depending on the intention of the planners—adds general or detailed information of the critical situation as it develops. The players are expected to formulate and take what they regard as appropriate actions to deal with each situation. The gaming exercise is essentially an intellectual challenge to the participants. Although the decision they make can put an emotional or mental strain on their ability as they seek to handle the critical incident they face, the participants do not find themselves in the setting of a real threat and conflict environment. The command post exercise ideally will provide added stressors if the actual decision makers are involved in it. However, this is often not the case, and therefore a realistic evaluation of the decision-making process may be flawed. In contrast, a full-scale simulation requires that all of the participants find themselves in a "real world" crisis environment that is almost indistinguishable from an actual situation. The setting—be it an office, airport, or refinery, for example—must be an actual potential target. Although the state of computer-generated environments has progressed remarkably since *Simulating Terrorism* was published in 1981, nonetheless a real facility must be used, with all its unique security challenges and vulnerabilities as well as those that are unexpected but will emerge during the simulation. In the conduct of the exercise, while the simulation to a certain degree needs to be staged to meet the security training requirements of the participating organizations, the setting is for all intents and purposes not a stage but the real world, whether the exercise originates in the cockpit of an actual aircraft or at the computer center that controls the flow of oil in a pipeline around the United States.

SIMULATIONS INVOLVE FAR MORE THAN ENGAGING IN ROLE PLAYING

In *Simulating Terrorism*, Sloan noted the importance of having all the participants go beyond simply assuming their respective roles so that they also "think and feel" the role they have taken. That suggestion has taken on even greater meaning as we seek to conduct simulations where there are particular roles that cannot be effectively played by "stand-ins," no matter how talented and skilled they may be, but must be undertaken by those individuals who would actually have to carry out the pertinent responsibilities in the case of an actual incident. Perhaps even more significantly, we need to be accurate in our portrayal of our adversaries. Given our growing knowledge of terrorists' attitudes and behavior and the need to create as realistic a perspective as possible, we could ideally use "reformed" terrorists, although that is unlikely for many reasons.[1] But one certainly could recruit those individuals with appropriate tactical skills who have been schooled in the "mindset" of the terrorists in order to very closely emulate their real-life counterparts. This ability to acquire the necessary "feel"—to mimic the belief system, values, attitudes, and other factors that help to shape the worldview of the terrorists, their motivations, and their actions—is addressed in more detail in chapters 5 and 6.

SIMULATIONS MUST BE A DYNAMIC AND LARGELY UNSCRIPTED PROCESS

The simulation technique has grown in complexity over the years. The simulations discussed in the original book were rather basic and inexpensive compared to the massive and very expensive regional and national exercises that now take place, often under the auspices of the Department of Homeland Security. But a hidden cost associated with these developments has exacerbated a trend that existed in earlier exercises: the tendency on the part of both the scenario builder and those who conducted the simulations to engage in too much scripting. In the early simulations, virtually every event was enunciated; the simulation description often started with "a hostage situation was initiated at 1600 at location X and ended with a successful or failed assault at 2400." The need for scripting, especially in more complex exercises, could be justified in part by the need to test many different aspects of the responses by the authorities, especially in a large-scale exercise. But overscripting took away the uncertainty and unpredictability that characterized the dynamics of an actual incident. In addition, the scripting also brought a sense of routine actions and reactions, particularly among those who had participated in multiple simulations. A largely unscripted process, in contrast, requires that participants adjust to the uncertainty and lack of predictability that accompanies an actual incident. In more than one overscripted simulation, the responding team was caught off guard by events that developed as a result of the interaction of the authorities and terrorists that were not part of the detailed scenario.

The need to improvise is vital and provides many training benefits. Bunker was involved in active-shooter training at a high school as a red team member. Tactical scenarios were conducted in a section of classrooms facing a common courtyard. The simulation background was that numerous calls had been made to the local police department informing them that shots had been fired at the high school. An ad hoc four-man police team quickly assembled in front of the high school and responded to the incident in a diamond tactical formation (point man, right and left flank, and rear guard). The officers, of course, focused on the classrooms off the courtyard and drew upon their past experiences with the behaviors of common criminals. The two red team trainers were allowed to improvise during the scenarios and continually challenged the responding officers by hastily setting up kill zones and firing positions, engaging in coordinated ambushes, and utilizing hit-and-run tactics. This included one of the trainers popping out of the heavy foliage at the end of the courtyard with an MP-5 submachine gun and spraying the responding officers moving past with sim-munitions. The intent was to show that the entire operational space was potentially dangerous and that terrorists would utilize all the nuances of the immediate terrain to their tactical advantage.

Responding Claremont Police officers deployed in a four-man (diamond formation) contact team during a simulated active-shooter incident at a high school in California. Courtesy of Gabriel Fenoy, *The Claremont Courier.*

SIMULATIONS ARE INCREASINGLY TOO COMPLEX IN COUNTERING THE LETHALITY OF SIMPLICITY

Given recent events, most notably 9/11 and the Mumbai attacks, there is certainly a valid concern that those involved in counterterrorism will have to learn to prevent or respond to operations that are more sophisticated than those that characterized the earlier days of terrorist incidents, in which a few hijackers, for example, could relatively easily defeat security measures, launch their assault, and seize the world's headlines. The fact remains, though, that in many instances, even if given general guidance and logistical support from a larger organization or network, the small combat cell of five to eight

Red team member with an MP-5 submachine gun hiding in cover prior to ambushing Claremont Police officers during a simulated active-shooter incident at a high school. Courtesy of Gabriel Fenoy, *The Claremont Courier.*

individuals still plan and ultimately conduct the operations. The speed and flexibility of these cells stands in stark contrast to the amount of time needed by simulation planners in preparing for complex simulations—and also the amount of lead time available to terrorists. In the early simulations presented in the original book, a combat cell could be organized and capable of initiating an attack within two days of the simulation being scheduled. That speed reflected the ability of small terrorist "red teams" to prepare and carry out their mission either independently or as part of a larger organization.

Today, as simulations become more complex, as the players become more numerous, and as the process of preparing for, conducting, and participating in an exercise becomes more elaborate, the potential ability of the terrorists to act quickly is forgotten or disregarded as meeting after meeting takes place among the simulators and those forces involved in the exercise to define their missions and the ever-increasing "rules of the game." An extreme case of this malaise was highlighted in Millennium Challenge 02: "The most elaborate war game the U.S. military has ever held was rigged so that it appeared to validate the modern, joint-service war-fighting concepts it was supposed to be testing, according to the retired Marine lieutenant general who commanded the game's Opposing Force."[2] Rather than allowing for free play of the opposing force (OPFOR), which initially crippled the U.S. operational naval forces, the fleet was "refloated," and only scripted play was then allowed by the red team. This same danger also exists in counterterrorism exercises.

In contrast to the simplicity and unity of action that continues to characterize the acts of the individual terrorists or the small combat cell, the organization and conducting of the simulation has in too many instances become bureaucratized, unfortunately mirroring the complex structures of the responding forces instead of the simplicity of the cell that adheres to the adage that "small is not only beautiful" but also, per their organizational doctrine, effective and lethal. Unfortunately, in contrast to the terrorists, the responses of those participating in the exercises (especially when these involve multiple organizations and forces) are characterized by not only a lack of unity of purpose but also bureaucratic competition that often leads to "gridlock and immobilization." As we shall see in chapter 7, there may be a need to simplify the terrorist attack cycle and compress the time that is required to execute all phases of it. Equally important is that those who are preparing or conducting simulations would be well advised to utilize the "small is beautiful" organizational doctrine of many terrorist groups, which unfortunately has proven to be all too effective against the cumbersome structure of our large-scale bureaucracies.

SIMULATIONS SHOULD NOT BE SUBJECT
TO THE TYRANNY OF OBSERVERS
OR POLITICIZED

A problem related to the danger of losing the dynamics necessary in a simulation is the emphasis on having too many observers at the scene of the exercise. There is no question that
observers are necessary to monitor and evaluate an exercise,
but for several reasons, they should be limited to an appropriate number and be largely unseen as the simulation takes
place. The presence of too many observers can lead to a situation in which there is an attempt, intentionally or uninten-
tionally, to overcontrol (often politically) and micromanage an
exercise, taking the dynamic aspects of the exercise out of the
hands of the direct participants; additionally, their existence
degrades the reality that the simulation should achieve. There
is nothing more disruptive when conducting a highly realistic
exercise than to have controllers highly visible and physically
designated by what they wear or by identification insignia.
This visual interference degrades the goal of having a simulation in which the line between actuality and training is effectively blurred and, if possible, essentially eliminated. Law
enforcement brass typically are unable to resist taking charge
during simulations and, if a simulation becomes a media
event, making a statement so as to look good on camera. Politicized simulations (even those internal to a department, such
as when the command staff shows up merely out of curios-
ity to observe a simulation) are detrimental to the functioning of the simulation and the training benefits being sought.
The dilemma is that often political backing is needed for the
tactical- or operational-level simulation to take place in the first
place. Attempts should be made to educate the politicized police officers, usually at the rank of captain or above in a large
department, of the detriments of bringing in excess observers.
A blanket dictate of "no rank exists during the simulation"

except for the organizational response functioning of the actual participants—such as the officer in charge (OIC) participating in the simulation—should be declared. In extreme cases of what may become a politicized event, the setting up of a media tent away from the simulation with refreshments and an assigned handler/briefer of the VIPs, departmental brass, and the press should be implemented.

SIMULATIONS SHOULD NOT MERELY EMPHASIZE WORST-CASE SCENARIOS

The tendency to develop scenarios to test the ability of federal counterterrorism organizations and forces is all too readily apparent in many contemporary simulations. While the threat of mass terrorism has become a reality, especially with the events of 9/11, the focus of many exercises today primarily deals with the threat and use of weapons of mass destruction (WMD). There is no question that incidents of mass terrorism and attacks associated with WMD are becoming more likely. But these are still the least likely weapons to be used. Attacks using conventional weapons and mass terrorism without resorting to WMD are still closer on the potential threat horizon. This consideration does not suggest that a focus on WMD in simulations should not continue; however, this focus should not occur at the expense of training forces to deal with the more likely conventional attacks, which may not take place in high-profile areas and will, first and foremost, require the effective handling of such incidents on the state and local level.

When one emphasizes high-visibility/high-casualty scenarios, the tendency is to primarily test the ability of the federal response while placing the state and local responses in a support mode, which ignores the reality that ultimately (with apologies to former Speaker of the House of Representatives Tip O'Neill for repurposing his phrase), "All terrorism is local."[3] That is, the first responders will in all likelihood come from the jurisdiction in which the attack occurs. The need for an emphasis on the "localization of counterterrorism simulations and training," therefore, should not be viewed as a secondary function. This "bottom up" perspective, along with a proactive and networked organizational approach, is the foundation upon which the terrorism early warning (TEW) groups have been built in Los Angeles and other U.S. cities. Although state and federal forces are valuable for their supporting role, any terrorist incident (short of a sustained terror campaign) will be long over by the time that out-of-area resources arrive. Additionally, although federal forces may be involved in criminal investigation and consequence management after a terrorist attack, they will not be involved in late-stage interdiction or immediate incident response. A prime example is the New York Police Department's last-minute early morning raid in Brooklyn in 1997 that interdicted a suicide bombing attack on the subway later that day by two Palestinian terrorists.[4]

Moreover, there is often an assumption that if one can deal with a "worst-case scenario," lesser cases will be easier to respond to. The problem here is twofold. First, with the exception of obvious cases of mass incidents, what could be viewed as profoundly disruptive at a local level (for example, an active shooting involving two or three casualties in a town or rural jurisdiction) would unfortunately be a relative common event in a high-crime urban area. Therefore, defining a "worst case" is difficult. Second, each incident differs, be it relatively small or large in scale. There is no reason to assume that because one can handle a major incident that there will somehow be an automatic transfer of skill to a smaller one. Indeed, if the smaller incident is not handled properly at the local level, it can readily escalate. Although not an act of terrorism, the brutal beating of Rodney King by police, which ignited a major civil disturbance, is a case in point. Care must therefore be taken to recognize an emergent danger but, concomitantly, not develop each simulation on the assumption that "the sky is falling."

SIMULATIONS SHOULD NOT BE PRIMARILY OR SOLELY REACTIVE IN NATURE

Most simulations officially start when an incident has been reported such as a bombing, hostage taking, or other form of terrorism. The emphasis in these exercises is primarily training and evaluating how well departments and other units respond to an attack. This was the approach essentially employed in the exercises noted in *Simulating Terrorism*. Over time, the responding forces were expanded to include a wide variety of first responders in addition to those in law enforcement or the military, but the simulations remained essentially reactive in part because of the emphasis on training to deal with hostage-taking situations. Even in these exercises, however, there was recognition of the need to provide a general means to test the ability of the targeted jurisdiction or organization to identify a potential threat. This pre-incident evaluation was particularly prevalent when working with military forces, who recognized and were trained in the requirements for operational security (OPSEC), that is, not to telegraph one's movements and therefore provide an adversary with vital tactical information but to raise the level of threat awareness so that unusual activities that might be part of a surveillance could be reported to the authorities. The simulations primarily conducted for police forces did not have as much of a pre-incident phase, in part because the departments often lacked or had only limited capability to engage in threat assessment, much less access to appropriate data related to existing groups and the threat environment. Nevertheless, there was an early awareness of the importance of the intelligence function, for, to paraphrase one counterterrorism official, "When there is a terrorist incident, there has been a 90 percent failure in counterterrorism measures, and that failure relates to the intelligence function."

The focus on intelligence may have been overly central to the earlier exercises, but in light of the tragic failures of intelligence that took place even before 9/11, there was a growing recognition of the need to develop a means to engage and test counterterrorism intelligence as an inherent aspect of a simulation. This was reinforced by acknowledgment of the fact that, particularly with the possibility for incidents of mass terrorism, the response, however effective, would in many ways be from the human, physical, and organizational damage control arenas, that is, consequence management. Testing the intelligence process was essential, for ultimately the most successful antiterrorism measures would involve preventing rather than responding to an attack. In chapter 7 and appendix 1, this vital role of incorporating the intelligence process (particularly with regard to collection, analysis, and dissemination) is discussed. In these days of increased levels of violence, authorities must move beyond a posture of reaction in dealing with prevention of terrorism and focus at least equally on preempting potential acts and campaigns of terror.

SIMULATIONS REQUIRE A CANDID AFTER-ACTION DEBRIEF

A block of time should always be allocated for a nonattribution debriefing period with all the participants involved to immediately talk about the simulation after it is completed. Even if everyone is exhausted, it is vital that the briefing begin while the participants are still in their roles and do not have time to intellectualize their experiences; if required, a more detailed briefing can be held later. The initial debriefing must be mandatory, as some personnel will have a tendency to run off to attend to their next professional obligation or cut out early to beat traffic home. To be fair to the participants, a reasonable time limit should be set for this debriefing, and the time limit should not be disregarded. All participants—including law enforcement officers, red team members, trainers, staff, and qualified observers—should provide their impressions. The press and anyone else not cleared to be in the debriefing must be excluded for OPSEC purposes, to ensure candid discussion and in order for the lessons learned to not become politicized. The debrief should not turn into a mutual admiration club meeting or a mass "pat on the back session" of how well the simulation went. Also, the danger always exists that the person who knows the least may attempt to talk the most, so the simulation coordinator must limit any one person from dominating the debrief. Preferably, the debriefing discussion should go round-robin with the top two or three observations from each participant or, even better, should cycle through the different participant categories, giving the most weight to the insights and reflections of the tactical and operational personnel actually being trained. The intent is to determine the lessons learned and identify what went right, what went wrong, and the counterterrorism implications that have resulted from the training.

A zero-defects mentality has no place in the debrief, nor does finger pointing or leveling any form of blame at others. Training operations have their own fog and friction, and typically more is learned from the mistakes made than the successes that serve to reinforce the status quo. Memories can be fragile and selective, so the ability to transcribe the verbal lessons learned or some sort of handout for short responses should be utilized to benefit the agency or response force being trained. The responses collected must be archived on a nonattribution basis. Bunker was once involved in an exercise where he was situated in a field command post and was figuratively wearing too many hats—providing red team injects to the incident OIC and monitoring the response, determining the red team's next course of action, and trying to use some of the injects to help test the utility of an innovative mapping technology being used by the responding command forces. One self-critique from that exercise was that another red team member was sorely needed in the command post so that better training could have been provided.

SIMULATIONS SHOULD INVOLVE THE IMPACTED COMMUNITY

It has been recognized for many years that acts of terrorism are ultimately aimed at an audience—be it a city, a country, a region, or internationally. This potential audience must be involved in simulations. The level of involvement, of course, will in part be determined by the size of the audience that would be affected by the incident. In conducting a simulation, community involvement is essential but often missing since the emphasis in the exercises frequently defines participants on the basis of their "official" involvement in countering terrorism. This omission has serious implications, for how a community copes with both threats and innocents will also determine the degree of individual and collective psychological impact ultimately created by terrorists. Moreover, if there is a level of terrorism awareness on the part of the public, if there is an understanding of the nature and goals of terrorists, the public will hopefully be less likely to overreact to an incident. This is extremely important because the "disruptive targeting" aspects of terrorism are typically overlooked by the response community. The psychic shockwaves that overwhelm a community with fear and ambiguity after the initial physical attack cause far more long-term damage than the actual use of the gun or the bomb. Further, a level of awareness can assist the authorities by having a public that will be involved in reporting potential suspicious behavior that might be a precursor to an act of terrorism. Admittedly, such awareness must be promoted in such a way as not to induce paranoia or dangerous stereotyping; for this reason, the public information officer (PIO) for the operational area, the terrorism liaison officer (TLO) from the jurisdictional intelligence center, and a community emergency response team (CERT) representative or their equivalents should be involved with simulation outreach. Fostering such awareness is nothing more than instituting a form of crime watch, a technique that has been effectively used to identify potential criminal activities before, while, or after they take place. Prominent unofficial community leaders should also be given an opportunity to participate in a simulation; local clergy and important business and civic leaders may have more credibility as informal spokespersons for their community than do public officials on the state and national level. Finally, such participation makes for a far larger group of stakeholders than those officials who are generally tasked with countering the threat and impact of terrorism.[5]

SIMULATIONS SHOULD NOT HAVE A CHECKLIST MENTALITY

Finally, in conducting simulations, there is often the desire to cover all contingencies. In so doing, one risks creating a checklist mentality. Such a mentality can have very negative effects on the conduct of a simulation, since it fails to take into account the changing dynamics and uncertainty that characterize an actual terrorist incident. Moreover, such a mentality and the accompanying rigidity it invites detract from the flexibility that is required not only to test the ability of the involved units, and when possible the community, but also to foster the capability of the red team to engage in highly realistic exercises. Ideally, a simulation—this point cannot be stated strongly enough—should as closely as possible approximate the physical, emotional, organizational, and tactical demands engendered by a real threat or attack.

CHAPTER 3

GUIDING THE SIMULATION

Planning is everything, plans are worthless!
—Helmuth von Moltke

In preparing for a simulation, many administrative details must be taken care of if the program is ultimately to be effective. There must be attention to detail, because even the most basic simulation calls for a good deal of planning to meet the training requirements of the sponsoring jurisdiction. Furthermore, although each exercise is open-ended, care must be taken to ensure effective safety and operational security (OPSEC) measures. A successful simulation entails a high degree of realism and tension at the corresponding tactical, operational, and/or political (decision-maker) level of training being implemented. There must be guidelines so that all participants recognize certain limits in their roles without sacrificing the uncertainty that should be inherent in each program.

In the evolution of each simulation, there is a concerted attempt to develop a scenario that will meet the training requirements of the participating departments or units. To properly guide a simulation, its mission and intent, organizational requirements, the actual administration of the simulation, and safety measures and OPSEC considerations must all be carefully thought out. The complexity of the simulation planning can range from the low end for basic active-shooter training through medium and high levels of complexity for combined small arms infantry assaults on facilities, hostage taking, and intelligence-focused simulations.

SIMULATION MISSION AND INTENT

The scenarios should be fashioned to meet the kind of threat the department anticipates in its jurisdiction. Thus, the selection of targets, attack methods, opposing force group, and accompanying demands, if applicable, are customized. This can be approached from diverse perspectives. While target(s), attack methods, and the opposing force (OPFOR) are always required, the original mission and intent of the simulation can initially be focused on a threat to a facility or venue (such as a sports arena or transit system), a certain type of tactical or operational threat (such as a suicide bombing or use of a rocket-propelled grenade), or a threat from a specific or general type of terrorist group (such as Al Qaeda or a white supremacist). Once the dominant simulation threat attribute is decided, then the two other threat attributes can be determined to support it. From the outside, these three components will, and should, appear seamless, but which one is originally decided upon ultimately drives simulation mission and intent.

This is a very different approach than was taken in the original *Simulating Terrorism* work, primarily because of changes in terrorism and conflict that have taken place in the past two to three decades. The original simulation technique utilized hostage taking for stage play–like purposes for the attack method and left wing and anarchist-type groups for the opposing force. The only attribute that was in question was the target set within a department's jurisdiction that was to be assaulted. For instance, in Tulsa, Oklahoma, the responding forces shared a concern that oil refineries within their jurisdiction were potential sites for incidents. In another simulation, the possible seizure of aircraft represented an ongoing concern among the authorities.

While methods of the initial assault varied—refineries, aircraft, and office buildings pose unique tactical requirements—the same basic stage play theme was followed. Still, it was and is recognized that the simulators must be sensitive to the local factors that condition responses in the participating jurisdiction. Certain local conditions remain constant and place various constraints on the responding forces irrespective of the kind of incident that is being simulated. The availability of targets, the composition and training of the participating units, and the administrative-political structures that would figure into an actual incident place important limits on the scenario.

Additional scenario questions then need to be asked. A basic question is, will the training focus on a pre-incident or transincident timeframe? Pre-incident scenarios are intelligence focused and are proactive in nature. Neutralization and interdiction of opposing forces at a safe house or in transit to the target may also be a component of the simulation. Transincident scenarios focus on the deployment of responding tactical and operational forces and opposing force engagement during the incident. Typically, postincident time frames are reserved for consequence management, recovery, investigative, and/or criminal intelligence exercises because at that point the needs of the injured and dead, physical destruction, denial of services, community shock and grief, and an active crime scene must be dealt with. In simulations that are more complex, a secondary or tertiary device or even a sniper may come into play during what the responders and investigators consider is the postincident phase of operations. Even more sophisticated simulations can witness a terrorist campaign in effect. This results in a number of incidents or tactical assaults taking place either near-simultaneously or over a much longer time frame. In these simulations, pre-incident, transincident, and postincident responses may be taking place simultaneously or in all manner of combinations within an operational area or law enforcement jurisdiction. A more advanced question is determining "where in" or "spanning what parts" of the attack cycle or attack cycles the training is focusing. (To better appreciate law enforcement interdiction and response requirements and needs, see chapter 7.)

The level of training being provided is also an important consideration. Is the training meant to be tactical, operational, or political (strategic) in nature? Different units and groups operate at different levels, whether law enforcement or military, within the line and block and command hierarchy. Questions here include who is being trained and why and is the training horizontal across a department (for example, for field officers only) or vertical up the chain of command (for example, from field response through the officer-in-charge). The length and complexity of the training will also have to be determined; this, in turn, will influence, or be influenced by, budget considerations. The most basic training can be conducted over the course of a few hours and cost a sponsoring agency almost nothing—just officer time, volunteer time (for role players and coordinators), and materials (sim-munitions). Such training "on the cheap" is not normally sustainable, however, if undertaken too often, and the quality and intensity of the training will always remain at the basic level. Higher levels of training can cost anywhere from thousands to tens of thousands to over a hundred thousand dollars, depending on the planning required, duration, and complexity of the training being provided. However, "throwing money at the problem" issues always exist, with governmental waste, bureaucratic interference, and contractor overcharging concerns. More money spent on a terrorist simulation does not always translate to superior training being provided.

Other basic considerations include what the red team will look like and who the role players will be (see chapter 5) and whether the training will be overtly scheduled ahead of time, with the location and schedule either made known to the trainees, coming as a partial surprise (sometime in this month you will undergo training), or coming as a complete surprise.

Different groups and agencies see pros and cons to different approaches with regard to who should know about counterterrorism training and when. Ultimately, no right or wrong approach exists; each perspective has tradeoffs, though for the sake of realism, actual training should be a complete surprise. If critical individuals are gone on vacation or are away at court and their loss negatively impacts local response capabilities, the void in expertise will simply have to be worked around. During the 9/11 attack, quite a few key members of the Los Angeles Terrorism Early Warning Group were in Salt Lake City, Utah, for an international conference on terrorism and did not get back to the operational area until early the next day. Still, a terrorism simulation exercise cannot be allowed to totally degrade daily operational capabilities, so compromises will have to be made.

The original *Simulating Terrorism* work promoted the ideal approach to scenario development. Once the framework of the scenario is agreed upon by the commanding officers of the police or military forces, the senior personnel are no longer involved in the development of the simulation if they are actually going to be in command of their forces when the incident is initiated. As in an actual crisis, they must develop their response without any prior knowledge of the terrorist assault. Cooperation with senior commanders is, of course, vital to ensure that the exercise meets the requirements of their departments, but the commanding officer, like his or her personnel, must be kept in the dark about the details of the impending operation if he or she is going to participate in the decision-making process once the simulation begins.

Also, the question must be asked whether the training will be made known to the public and press prior to or after the training is conducted or whether the training will remain "close hold" information. Sometimes goodwill is sought with the public after the training is conducted to make the community feel safer—with an article or television news story run about it—and also as an open deterrent to terrorists: this community is a hard target, so beware. Simulation training and other security measures make venues and communities more hardened to attack, as opposed to the vulnerable and soft targets that terrorists prefer to assault. A good example of this fact is the case of Buford Furrow, a white supremacist, who shot up a Jewish community center in August 1999 after deciding against attacks directed at more well known Jewish venues because of their higher levels of security. Other times, sensitive tradecraft is being utilized openly during the training (for example, bomb squads are normally very concerned about OPSEC), so no outside observers or taping of the exercise will be allowed.

Many times, the above considerations will have to be tempered and modified to obtain and retain command staff and community support for the simulation. The logic of counterterrorism operations and local response at the tactical and operational levels is not always synonymous, and in fact sometimes is at odds, with the perceptions and needs of the department brass, politicians, and community leaders. For some high-profile simulations and programs, a multimonth process may be required to get stakeholder "buy in" for the training to take place. This is often a requirement in affluent communities, heavily politicized ones, and those with high levels of citizen participation in local governance. In other communities, this process is either not needed or can be dramatically shortened. Such public and policing policy extremes are not that unusual. Both authors know of communities that exist side by side but because of local politics have 180-degree-difference requirements for training and program implementation.

SIMULATION ORGANIZATIONAL REQUIREMENTS

The devil is always in the details, and the more planning for a simulation the better—with the caveat that at some juncture a "saddle point" is reached, which means that at a certain point the time spent on additional planning yields only marginal training benefits. Bureaucratic groups should not be allowed to take charge of exercise planning, because unnecessary meetings will likely be scheduled and provide no tangible returns. Exercise planning should always be under the control of the training groups in coordination with the law enforcement agency or military unit being trained. Planning, logistics, personnel, funding, equipment, communication, and command and control issues all fall under the umbrella of the components required to put a simulation together.

Meetings, either minimal (that is, over the course of hours) or more extensive (that is, over the course of days or spread over weeks), with the training stakeholders will be required depending on the type of simulation and the level of complexity that is being planned for. An officer from the group being trained is typically selected to act as a liaison to assist the group in obtaining the equipment, selecting personnel, and making other preparations for the attack. Only the liaison officer will be given a copy of the simulation operations order, which is restricted, so that he or she can assist the group in meeting the pre-exercise requirements. Security in the development of each simulation is vital, and distribution of the operations order is strictly on a need-to-know basis. The liaison officer is essential also because of the wide variety of requirements that must be attended to before the simulation can be successfully executed. In the case of larger-scale simulations, liaison officers will be required from different participating agencies or even groups within a major metropolitan police department such as special weapons and tactics (SWAT) teams, hazardous materials (HAZMAT) personnel, bomb squads, intelligence units, and counterterrorism bureaus.

The date and time when the simulation takes place can also take on symbolic or meaningful importance. Certain dates—such as April 19, which was the final act of the Waco siege, and

April 20, which was Adolf Hitler's birthday—have great significance for extremist groups. Different months of the year also have diverse weather conditions and occupancy patterns for targeted venues. The same goes for time of day, with shift changes, vacations, and even wind patterns and different microclimates (for example, the morning could be foggy and have an eastern wind pattern while the afternoon might be clear and have a western wind pattern). Weather conditions are extremely important for WMD intelligence–driven exercises because the exact time of an intervention into a safe house with a WMD will determine where HAZMAT contamination will end up if the mission is a failure and thus necessitate more or less pre-interdiction neighborhood evacuation as a precautionary measure.

When candidate locations for both single- and multiple-venue exercises are generated and then narrowed down, the ground needs to be physically walked at some point with the locals. Pictures and videos are no substitute for actually going over the operational space and understanding where the kill zones, blind spots, avenues of approach, and other spatial relationships of influence are within the defined terrain. The simulation designers can then determine which candidate location or locations or which specific locations within a larger venue—such as an amusement park, parade route, or large facility—would be the best place to undertake the training. The actual ground should be looked at from both the responding law enforcement (or military) force and red team perspectives. The one caveat is that the actual red team members should not be allowed information and insights beyond what their terrorist personas should know about the targeted venue: trusted insider knowledge beyond what the threat group should know will influence their behavior and actions during the actual planning and execution of the simulated assault. Because manpower is usually stretched for terrorist simulations, sometimes red team leaders will participate in the initial simulation design and will have to remember to compartmentalize and not draw upon the insider information that they are privy to. Other red team members should always be treated in a need-to-know manner from the start to maintain appropriate terrorist cell operational security that will make their participation in the simulation far more realistic.

Sometimes the training cannot take place at the actual venue being targeted. This is a situation that should be avoided whenever possible, but in some instances (because of political or operational factors) this artificiality of the training becomes a necessity. A case in point would be a SWAT and bomb squad response to a bus rigged with explosives full of hostages in a busy urban intersection. The actual tactical assault and render-safe component of the exercise may have to be done in another location, with all of the exercise terrain modeling and response information played as if the simulation were taking place at the actual intersection.

The most important part of simulation organization is the creation of the exercise plan (ExPlan). This document provides an overview of the simulation, explains the planning process, and delineates the resources required to put on the simulation. These plans have to be treated as critical infrastructure or law enforcement sensitive in nature because of the information that they contain. These are artificial restrictive designations (a nonfederal classification) placed on the document for OPSEC requirements so that the plan is kept secured and hopefully not obtained by the media, the public, or, worse, those with malicious intent. Having an ExPlan fall into the hands of the wrong people would be detrimental to the well-being of a community, the targeted venue or venues, and the local law enforcement and response agencies.

Very detailed plan templates exist but are either restricted or proprietary in nature and cannot be provided in public documents. The official U.S. source for developing such exercises is the Homeland Security Exercise and Evaluation Program (HSEEP; https://hseep.dhs.gov). This publicly accessible Web site has exercise development booklets, training courses, and other resources readily available. It also contains the HSEEP Toolkit, described as "an interactive, on-line system for exercise scheduling, design, development, conduct, evaluation and improvement planning." Access to this toolkit, however, is restricted, and it is available only to vetted law enforcement and responder agencies. The restricted FBI's Law Enforcement Online Information Sharing Network also has a real-time Internet-based tool called Virtual Command Center (VCC; http://www .leo.gov) that is being utilized by some agencies for exercise purposes. The U.S. military services also have their own computerized scenario and mission support software programs. A generic and somewhat more inclusive ExPlan would contain the following categories:[1]

> *Exercise Information:* The time, date, and location of the simulation and how long it will take place.
>
> *Goals:* The statement that such-and-such counterterrorism training will take place and what the benefits will be.
>
> *Objectives:* The delineation of what will actually be evaluated or assessed in the training.
>
> *Narrative:* The storyline that the simulation is following, with various levels of detail possible. This storyline can be very basic, such as having local police respond to shots fired at an elementary school, with ad hoc teams forming in front of the school, drawing weapons, and tactically advancing onto the school grounds to provide assistance and if need be neutralize any active-shooter threats to the students, faculty, and staff. More-detailed narratives can include a discussion of global news events and indications and warnings (I&W) leading up to the simulation or, for still

more detail, can draw upon a stand-alone MSEL (master scenario events list). For simulation purposes, the less rigid the exercise the better.

Participants: An overview of who is involved in the simulation: coordinators, agency liaisons, and referees; the aggressors (red team), the responders (blue team), and the hostages/neutral role players; and official observers, technology support personnel, facility stakeholders, miscellaneous individuals such as those videotaping the event for training purposes, and in some rare instances the press.

Exercise Command and Control: A description of how the simulation will be run, how information flows and is managed, and who has authority and control over the various components of the simulation.

Red Team Plan: An explanation of what the red team mission is and how they are going to obtain it. This item can be hasty and oral, given in a frag (fragment) order that basically outlines the five W's (who, what, where, when, and why) of the task to be accomplished.[2] Other plan approaches can be drawn from general orders pertaining to Special Operations Forces and a five-paragraph order or O-SMEAC (orientation, situation, mission, execution, administration/logistics, command/signal). The danger always exists that the OPFOR are given too much rationality and Western cultural bias in their tactical and operational thinking, so their modus operandi must be precisely matched to their simulated field activities.

Blue Team Plan: A declaration of the responding department, agency, or interagency operational procedures and practices to be followed by the blue team in their interdiction and response planning. State and federal guidelines may vary, but the incident command system (ICS), defined in the National Incident

Management System (NIMS), is becoming standard. Military response protocols and rules of engagement follow different guidelines.

Equipment List: A checklist of items—from small arms, body armor, IEDs, and booby traps, handcuffs, and hoods through vehicles and communications gear—that may be required. This is dependent on the equipment needs of the actual type of simulation being undertaken.[3]

Safety and Security Measures: A description of how the participants in the simulation and local residents in the community will be protected from harm during the course of the exercise. This section will also ensure OPSEC requirements and delineate what protocols to follow in case of an injury to a participant.

Evaluation Method: The specific type of feedback loop chosen to critique the training that was provided, the law enforcement response, and the lessons learned from that training to make local counterterrorism and school safety protocols and response more effective.

Ad Hoc: A list of final planning considerations focused on items satisfying human bodily needs, such as food, water, shade, sunscreen lotion, and mosquito repellent, and miscellaneous items such as dry erase pens, batteries, cell phone chargers, a small first aid kit for injuries, and the like. Nothing is worse than having a laptop run down its batteries and then find out that no hard copies of the ExPlan exist and the only digital plan in the command post was on that laptop, which is now out of service. Plan for redundancy and expect technology to fail.

Very detailed simulations will typically have a situation manual (SitMan), the controller and evaluator (C/E) handbook, exercise evaluation guides (EEGs), and numerous appendixes that include such topics as glossaries of terms, acronyms, listings of items, and points of contact. Although not needed for simpler intra-agency simulations, such glossaries can be very important for more-complex endeavors that are interagency where the responding forces do not speak the same operational and bureaucratic language. A great example pertaining to this issue can be seen in interagency operations during the Los Angeles riots of 1992:

> Police officers responded to a domestic dispute, accompanied by marines. They had just gone up to the door when two shotgun birdshot rounds were fired through the door, hitting the officers. One yelled "cover me!" to the marines, who then laid down a heavy base of fire. . . . The police officer had not meant "shoot" when he yelled "cover me" to the marines. [He] meant . . . point your weapons and be prepared to respond if necessary. However, the marines responded instantly in the precise way they had been trained, where "cover me" means provide me with cover using firepower. . . . Over two hundred bullets [were] fired into that house.[4]

This incident could have been a major tragedy because the wife and children of the suspect who had fired the shotgun blast were inside the house. Luckily, no one in the house was injured from the Marines' covering fire. This incident provides a strong case for the need for common terminology and even concepts of operation to be spelled out in appendixes for some simulation exercises.

ADMINISTERING THE SIMULATION

Derived from the command and control section of the ExPlan will be the instructions concerning how the simulation will be run. A document delineating specific roles, responsibilities, and the authorities (what they are in charge of) will be given to the exercise controller, referees, safety officer, and other support personnel. A simulation organizational chart may or may not be needed, depending on the size and complexity of the training. If it is department training–based and involving a small organization or tactical unit, all of the officers will know each other and a formal diagram of some sort will probably not be required. With added personnel, the inclusion of outside participating players, and increased complexity of the operations, a well-articulated organizational chart and span of control requirements may be needed.

Some sort of site or location will be required to coordinate and implement the simulation. Typically, this is next to or in a corner of the responding blue team command post. Once again, this is simulation dependent and can range from the trunk of a car, a truck tailgate, or a card table to a grouping of tables in a facility or tent to an actual control room or venue of some sort. Tracking and management of the exercise can be done via pen, paper, and whiteboard; laptop and static computer equipment; or collaboration Web sites. Hard line and cell phones can be used for communication purposes from the control site to the field and other venues. Runners may also be used for passing notes, documents, or verbal instructions. Other forms of communication may include e-mails, instant messaging, texting, and even whistles or loudspeakers for field use. Predesignated venues or areas also need to be defined for the red team if a control element is utilized (for example, if a command cell is coordinating multiple assault teams out in the field), for the observers to be located, and for resting and predeployment response forces, and as well as where the walking wounded should be taken care of (such as those suffering from sprained ankles, fatigue, and dehydration). The location of and provisions made for water, food, first aid, and rest rooms need to be considered and designated, along with other miscellaneous supplies.

All simulations will progress through three basic phases, much like a simple terrorist incident: presimulation (before), transsimulation (during), and postsimulation (after). These phases are required to take place sequentially, and none of them may be overlooked or intentionally skipped.

The presimulation phase gets all the participating personnel in their appropriate places and mindsets. A presimulation brief is given; this brief, which can provide some basic guidance and intent, can be read off a paper or delivered by means of a PowerPoint presentation. Handouts may or may not be used. The simulation is walked through for all the participants and observers with housekeeping rules (such as what to do in case of personal or family emergencies) being provided along with safety protocols, simulation boundaries (that is, in play and out of play areas), participant locations, and other exercise criteria. Weapons and other equipment are also given last-minute functioning checks, the agreed-upon method of starting and ending the simulation is made known to the participants, and everyone gets into their positions.

Once the appropriate agreed-upon means is used to begin the simulation, the transsimulation phase is entered. The actual training exercise is played out either in real time or under compressed time guidelines. Because the transsimulation phase is the focus of much of this work, it should go smoothly—but something will always come up and Murphy will try to degrade the effectiveness and optempo (operational tempo) of the exercise (see chapter 4). During this phase, the red team and blue team plans are implemented, role players representing hostages and victims play their part, and the controllers, referees, and observers undertake their duties.

The postsimulation phase is entered when the agreed-upon stand-down order ending the simulation is given to the participants. The response forces are not to know when the simulation is to be ended ahead of time. The head of the jurisdiction and the simulation director will determine the actual time when the simulation is ended. This is when the nonattribution hot-wash (after-action debrief) is given to all the participants and observers, who will have been assembled together in a common area. Past experience has shown that the initial debrief should be given as soon as possible after the conclusion of the exercise. If more than an hour passes before the debrief takes place, the simulation participants will be totally out of their roles and will intellectualize their responses. Lessons learned and implications for training, doctrine, and response should be discussed, along with candid performance critiques and suggestions to make future simulations better. A full debrief can take place later. Cleanup and policing of the facility or venues for trash and other debris as well as securing weapons, equipment, and the facility used for the simulation are also done during this stage.

The above sequencing and exercise attributes are common to all simulations and represent a basic training event. Many simulations will add in additional front end, middle, and/or back end components to their exercises. No right or wrong method exists in this regard; such additional components will be decided upon due to local politics, training preferences and needs, the desired complexity of the exercise that will be undertaken, planning time, and money factors. Front end components would include read- or view-ahead packages for the responders; personal biographies written by red team members enabling them to better get into their roles; a detailed attack plan prepared by the red team after they have made a virtual and physical reconnaissance of the targeted venue; and a combination of playbooks, mission folders, and intelligence preparation for operations (IPO) planning for the blue team, potentially including an early Cold Start in which intelligence (both useful and deceptive) is provided to the blue team weeks or months in advance via an MSEL list to get them slowly warmed up for the simulation. Middle components to a simulation may bring in some sort of advanced technology demonstration (ATD) or new form of doctrine or training to be tested. Technology examples would include computer terrain simulators with real-time camera portals for mission planning and responder life vests with GPS location and health monitoring, while new doctrine would include implementing different tactical formations for terrorist response or actively practicing head shots against suicide bomber threats. Back end components may include a formal Participant Evaluation Packet (typically mandated when federal monies have been utilized), the creation of written reports and lessons-learned documents, and the development of departmental and interagency training tapes edited from raw footage taken during the simulation.

SAFETY MEASURES AND OPERATIONAL SECURITY

Safety and security issues must always be considered when developing and implementing a terrorist or school violence simulation. A balance must be sought between realistic training and these two issues and also when the real world and the simulated-environment play interfere with one another. Elements of these issues and interactions include physical safety; potential for psychological and emotional duress; departmental, venue, and tradecraft OPSEC requirements; local criminal and questionable participant activities; family, natural, and man-made disasters and crises; and other factors such as general liability and departmental concerns.

The physical safety component of the simulation process is generally based on local and individual state departmental protocols for law enforcement and federal protocols (not always in sync) for the FBI, DEA, ATF, and military services. In the case of training in California, Cal/OSHA (Division of Occupational Safety and Health) mandates could come into effect. For federal requirements, OSHA (Occupational Safety and Health

Administration) guidelines would be consulted. For this reason, it is best to consult with the agency or departmental safety officer when planning a simulation that will take place in the field. Many times, law enforcement safety guidelines will be far different from those pertaining to the fire and rescue services. A basic tension will always exist between promoting realism by simply sensitizing all participants to basic safety measures and following an overly bureaucratic checklist or operational requirements approach that destroys any semblance of realism taking place in the simulation. The middle ground between realism and safety can be a fine line. Bunker was involved in Level C (chemical suit, gloves, and filter) training a few years back for mass decontamination and force protection purposes with fire safety and SWAT officers at an airport facility. A small tactical red team made an assault on the mass decontamination unit, and members of the red team who were captured and arrested had to be fully decontaminated before being processed. As part of the training exercise, all those participants wearing Level C gear, including Bunker, had to undergo pre- and postsimulation screening and monitoring of vital signs, and protocols were explained so that participants would recognize whether they or others became overheated (as some participants, even those in top physical condition, did).

Restricted access using tape, sentries, and other exclusionary means to simulation venues is required to ensure the safety of all participants and observers, especially when sim-munitions, blanks, paintballs, fishing line and wire booby trap triggers, or flash bangs or other pyrotechnics are being utilized. Understanding and planning for medical response and transport needs and the locations of local hospitals are also important. In the case of some very large simulations, paramedics and an ambulance may even be on hand as a resource just in case an injury of some sort takes place.

A major focus of the original *Simulating Terrorism* work was on mental duress issues and the psychological safety of those

View of SWAT personnel in Level C protective gear deployed in front of a MODEC mass decontamination unit during a terrorism training exercise at a Southern California airport. This was an early law enforcement exercise that focused on providing force protection capabilities to a decontamination unit and its personnel deployed in the field. Courtesy of Robert Bunker, Counter-OPFOR Corporation.

being taken hostage in the exercises. Guidelines for the potential hostages were kept simple and explicit to avoid any potential misunderstandings:

> The participants are told that, if they are seized, under no circumstances should they attempt to employ force to effect their escape. They are cautioned not to fake either a physical or [a] mental breakdown as a means of attempting to be released from captivity. They are notified that, if an emergency does take place, it has been preplanned and acted out by selected persons, who are thus testing the response of the authorities and the terrorists to the crisis. A clear warning is given that, if an undesignated

SWAT personnel in Level C protective gear holding simulated weapons at an airport mass decontamination training exercise. Referees and cameraperson also evident. Courtesy of Robert Bunker, Counter-OPFOR Corporation.

individual fakes an illness, it must be assumed that the emergency is real: the simulation will consequently have to be temporarily suspended or terminated. That requirement is essential because, even though the would-be hostages are in good physical condition, there is no guarantee that physical and mental difficulties will not be experienced by some of them, given the levels of stress that are incorporated into the exercises. Despite the warning, in a number of simulations there was the possibility of over-reaction by the hostages who thought that one of their fellow victims was ill even though intellectually they knew that the emergency was preplanned. Because of the potentially dangerous emotional responses among individuals in the target group, the simulation director and an observer constantly monitored the emotional climate in the barricaded area during the simulation. If tensions became too intense, the lead terrorist reduces the level of intimidation experienced by the hostages.[5]

More specifics on the dynamics of hostage taking should be consulted in the original work, as this is one area of discussion and analysis that has stood well the test of time and the changing patterns of terrorist activities.

Operational security considerations must always be considered when engaging in counterterrorism simulations. OPSEC is a well-known military concept but has been less understood and less frequently practiced by law enforcement; it is even more alien to the fire, health, and other responder groups. Specialized law enforcement units, however, such as intelligence, dedicated counterterrorism units, and bomb squads and HAZMAT units are especially aware of the need for OPSEC and the use of secure communications. Documents pertaining to the exercise, response capabilities and techniques, and training shortfalls and lessons learned all have varying degrees of sensitivity attached to them. The Federal Law Enforcement Training Center (FLETC) offers an OPSEC course, but very few U.S. law enforcement personnel have been trained in this area, so some rudimentary principles need to be gone over before engaging in a simulation. Closing off the exercise venue—as discussed earlier for physical safety needs—also has the added benefit of keeping the press and tourists away, but having an individual or an element tasked with countersurveillance duty is always prudent to ensure that the simulation and the blue team response are not being monitored and photographed. In real-life incidents, surveillance, communications monitoring, and even communications jamming do take place. During an operation in San Diego during the "Biodevastation protests," undercover law enforcement personnel were photographed and their images placed on an Anarchist-affiliated Web site supporting the protests. The red teams in the original terrorism simulations constantly exploited OPSEC vulnerabilities of the responding law enforcement units by monitoring their radio communications. The bad guys were typically well informed about the enviable armed assault that came with the same pattern being repeated time and again by different responding forces across the simulations.

Also, moles and unauthorized personnel can occasionally weasel their way into an exercise. Therefore, vigilance is required not only on the exercise perimeters but also inside of what are considered secured areas. For Bunker, this fact hit home when he was attending a terrorism exercise focusing on a HAZMAT device placed within a facility. In that incident, a new student in a university program the author was then teaching was helping to advise the exercise! The student had not been vetted to observe the exercise, much less been determined qualified to give advice, and had sweet-talked his way into an advisory role. After some phone calls and investigation, the individual was shut out of future local counterterrorism response involvement.

Simulations and training taking place in public venues such as in downtown city areas and tourist hot spots also have the potential to both come in contact with actual criminal activities and trigger concerns by sharp-eyed civilians, security guards, and police officers in response to questionable activities being undertaken by the participants. Surveillance and reconnaissance of facilities by red teams and countersurveillance by the blue team means that a lot of eyeballs and sensing equipment are focusing on the surrounding streets, avenues of approach, and actual facility or complex itself. Normal patterns start to make themselves apparent, as do anomalies. Drug dealing, prostitution, theft, or even robbery or more serious crimes may be uncovered or witnessed. Protocols have to be in place to report such activity to the simulation controllers and the proper local authorities. In cases of immediate threat of bodily injury, simulation play will have to be suspended and the situation dealt with. Additionally, simulation participants (specifically, the red and blue team members) may engage in actions and behaviors that will get them reported to the local police or even approached and questioned by locals informally or in an official capacity. Bad surveillance techniques, entering vacant units for observation purposes, clumsy human engineering attempts, and the purposeful probing of off-limits and restricted areas may all trigger such concerns. Typically, cover stories can be utilized to mask such activities and keep the operatives out of trouble, but sometimes referees or handlers may have to intercede. If all else fails for simulations taking place in public venues, a "safe word" should be provided and confirmed with the jurisdictional law enforcement agency, which shall have been made aware of and briefed on the training being undertaken.

Sometimes personal and family emergencies and real-world natural and man-made disasters will take place prior to or even during a simulation. These will always have to take priority over the needs and requirements of the simulation, with some personnel not being available to participate or the entire exercise being put on hold or even cancelled. In some instances when the timing of such simulations and disasters have overlapped, a golden opportunity has been achieved: the local responders are already either in or close to their positions and units, and subject-matter experts are on hand who can be tasked for futures (enemy intent), analysis and synthesis, and consequence management cells to support an enhanced operational response that would not normally exist.

Other concerns influencing simulations are general liabilities due to participant and observer injury; facility, equipment, and rental car damage; the use of legal disclaimers and medical releases; and the ever-present potential for lawsuits. While such concerns will not typically influence the actions of public agencies, sometimes liability release documents must be signed for outside participants, and individuals and companies providing simulation training have to be cognizant of potential litigation and general liability issues. Public organizations and departments also have to ensure that the simulation does not jeopardize goodwill with the community, and these organizations may have to enact policy disclaimers and nonendorsement of products or services as an agreed-upon element of the training that will be undertaken. Bureaucratic concerns and infighting may also be trigged during the implementation phase of a simulation, and a few simple response contingencies should be thought out. In a perfect world, all the good guys come together to protect our citizens from the bad guys. Our world is far from perfect. This is just part of the human condition, and unfortunately in some cases the criminals and terrorists work far better together than do the law enforcement and responder agencies—especially in political and bureaucratic arenas.

CHAPTER 4

MURPHY'S LAW
CAN PROVE FATAL

There was a failure in counterterrorism intelligence.
—A common finding in after-action reports

As in many aspects of life, Murphy's Law ("If it can go wrong, it will go wrong") has applicability to both simulations and responding to actual incidents. Unfortunately, the end result can lead to death and destruction. Good planning and simulations can identify miscalculations and their causes. Ideally, in the evaluation process, necessary changes can be made to lessen or eliminate errors from being repeated. No matter how demanding the simulations, however, each training exercise or actual event takes on unique dynamics. A combination of the environment in which the crisis occurs, the behavior of all the participants (ranging from the security forces to the victims and terrorists), technological challenges, and fortune all determine the dynamics and the outcome.

Ultimately, there are no fail-safe means to totally eliminate errors, especially in the superheated atmosphere that accompanies a demanding simulation or an incident of terrorism. But analysis of past simulations and incidents can identify patterns of miscalculation that may differ from one crisis to another but are similar to each other. Moreover, if the personal, organizational, and tactical skills are based on demanding preparation, Murphy's Law may still be operative, but the probability of the law taking effect can be lessened or at least minimized, to the point that it has no negative effect on the outcome. One way to analyze the patterns of miscalculations is to attempt to analytically walk through the experiences drawn from past simulations or actual incidents. This can be a very crooked and often unpredictable walk, but the identified patterns can act as a compass in the preparation of new exercises and responding to future crises.

"IT CAN'T HAPPEN HERE" SYNDROME

When the first simulations were conducted by the study group on international terrorism, there was (with some exceptions— most notably in Europe and Israel) a lack of actual experience in dealing with threats and acts of terrorism. Certainly, domestic relations disputes, abortive robberies, and other forms of criminal violence could be found on the police logs of many jurisdictions, and recognition of the need to develop negotiation teams and tactical teams to deal with these events was growing. But (especially in the United States) terrorism remained something that affected other people in other places or, in the case of the United States, occurred mostly in large urban areas on the East and West Coast. As a result, particularly in simulations where local authorities were confronted with the first testing of their ability to respond to terrorist incidents, the local police dispatcher was often reluctant to accept the reality of the situation. Had it been a robbery or other conventional act, the response might have been quicker, but when the call was received there were questions as to whether the police were dealing with a prank call or another form of false alarm.[1] This view, in the absence of an overt act witnessed by the police or the public, could delay response time when a rapid reaction might be crucial. A patrol car could be sent out to ascertain whether there was an actual event, but the reluctance to initiate immediate action often set the stage for an initial error in dealing with an act of terrorism.

Certainly the response would be quicker on various military bases both in the United States and overseas where force protection measures were in place, but even then the need for verification of a potential hoax delayed response time, especially on domestic bases. The notable exception to this was evident for especially sensitive installations, where a quick reaction did take place—for example, on what were then called Strategic Air Command (now STRATCOM) bases, where the security of nuclear weapons was paramount. For most local police forces, however, terrorism stood at the low end of the threats and actions with which they were concerned. The first bombing of the World Trade Center in 1993 should have been a warning that terrorism would escalate in the United States. But to those in the "heartland," terrorism essentially remained a relatively remote problem affecting both coasts.

All this changed with the bombing of the Federal Building in Oklahoma City on April 19, 1995. The headlines read "Terrorism Comes to the Heartland," and there was finally awareness that no area was "zoned" against terrorism. Local jurisdictions, in conjunction with federal agencies, finally started to engage in threat assessments on the local level and to develop counterterrorism capabilities. Not until the events of 9/11, however, did the country finally start to more fully mobilize to the threat after the fact. As a result, especially with the formation of the Department of Homeland Security, the previous underreaction to terrorism was followed by a predictable overreaction as the national government initially threw money at the problem in preparing for acts of terrorism. The "It can't happen" syndrome was largely replaced by the "It could happen" syndrome, in which very uneven but heavy funding was provided based not on a systematic threat assessment but on a classic form of pork barrel legislation. Small departments began to be given equipment that they could not or, in all likelihood, would not use, and larger departments increasingly developed capabilities, for better or worse, that rivaled those on the national level. As

It *can* happen here: training is best conducted when it is cost-effective, simple, sustainable, and free of politics and overbureaucratization. In this active-shooter exercise photo, U.S. Air Force Staff Sgt. Diana Irish, a training instructor for the 305th Security Forces Squadron (SFS), shows a room-clearing technique to Master Sgt. George Hamilton during active-shooter training on McGuire Air Force Base, New Jersey, on January 17, 2008. The training is designed to prepare SFS personnel in responding to a shooting incident in a school or work center. Courtesy of U.S. Air Force, photograph by Kenn Mann (released).

a result, simulations now are likely to involve a faster response time, but because of high-profile exercises, the dispatcher in all likelihood will believe that a genuine threat is a simulation and not the real thing. "This is only a drill" may have replaced "It can't happen here."

"I'VE GOT A SECRET" SYNDROME

Another of the reasons for the "It can't happen here" syndrome in the early days of simulations and terrorism was based on the fact that although international terrorism was increasingly a major target for intelligence on the national level, it did not take priority in state and local law enforcement jurisdictions. Police at these levels had their hands full with gleaning basic police intelligence in regard to a wide variety of criminal behavior and the ever-continuing concern over drug traffic. With the exception of some major departments, state and local police often lacked the interest, capability, and analytical staff to collect and analyze threats and acts of terrorism.[2]

Moreover, as in the case of police intelligence in general, whatever information was acquired was largely of a tactical versus a strategic nature. Even with regard to domestic extremists, local police primarily relied on the Federal Bureau of Investigation (FBI) and other national agencies to assess and act on threats. If the first World Trade Center bombing acted as a wake-up call for the national intelligence community to place more emphasis on counterterrorism intelligence, this awareness unfortunately did not lead to identifying and fixing the problem with regard to sharing information and acquiring actionable intelligence that might have helped to prevent 9/11. Thus, in both simulations and dealing with actual incidents, it was not surprising that state and local departments did not appreciate the key role played by intelligence in preventing and responding to acts and campaigns of terrorism. Consequently, in the early simulations, the rather general threat assessment provided to the participating departments was not enough to test their ability to analyze and disseminate information throughout their organizations.

As noted earlier, the Oklahoma City bombing opened the eyes of the authorities to local threats and was an impetus to the development of the sharing of intelligence from the national to the state and local levels. Joint terrorism task forces (JTTFs) and all-source fusion centers have certainly been steps in the right direction. But a problem arose then, and it still remains. These efforts were primarily led by the FBI, and local police often felt that the sharing of intelligence was one-way because the bureau would perceived as obtaining local intelligence but not reciprocating. Although the mutual sharing of information has improved, there are still problems, especially the concern that the sharing of intelligence on the local level could reveal sensitive sources and methods with respect to domestic and foreign collection of information.[3]

Security classifications and this compartmentalization have acted as a barrier to an integrated effort. The problems of acquiring and disseminating intelligence are even more crucial today, given the nature of the expanded terrorist threat; future simulations will need to much more clearly test the ability of all organizations involved in counterterrorism to acquire the information they need. Earlier exercises showed all too clearly that even when information was available it was not shared, because of the lack of integration and an unwillingness to provide intelligence in a complex intelligence community within which information means power. The "I've got a secret" syndrome still hampers the acquisition and sharing of intelligence.[4] Consequently, in later simulations and workshops, more emphasis needed to be placed on testing the intelligence process of the participating organizations in terms of both longer-term strategic threats and shorter-term tactical requirements. (The means by which the intelligence process can be best evaluated can be found in appendix 1.)

"I'M IN CHARGE HERE" SYNDROME

Two themes in this book directly relate to organizational and behavioral stress at the outset of and the duration of a simulation. First, ultimately all terrorism is local: that is, whether it be a domestic or an international incident, the local authorities and their police and security forces will in all likelihood be the first responders. Second, because terrorism is a form of asymmetric conflict, the best response should incorporate the small size and outward simplicity of terrorist organizational structures.[5] With regard to the former, in numerous simulations (even if they involved a relatively small single department) there was often the problem of command and control after the police arrived. At first, the response tended to be slow and exhibited little forethought, and the focus after initial contact was primarily to establish a perimeter. When the high profile of the incident became clear to the department, mid- and then senior-level officers would add their numbers to the first responders. This initial crush of personnel often made it difficult to quickly establish command and control. The situation was often exacerbated with the fact that unless a mobile command post was quickly available or a central command post was established to help direct the on-scene commander, the crowded environment of a temporary site not equipped with adequate jacks for communication and electrical power for equipment would start to degrade the capability of the responders as time went on.

Moreover, when a command post was finally established, moving to it often detracted from whatever initial rhythm to diffuse the situation was in place. The problem was further amplified when mid- and senior-level command officers, instead of relying on their specialized units and relatively trained specialists, ran the risk of micromanaging a situation that, irrespective of their rank, they were not trained to deal with. In addition, in more than one instance, even if the initial response team was effectively dealing with the situation at various military bases, the base commander or an even more senior officer would seek to intrude on operations. The creation of a situation in which there was a growing issue of who was in charge was certainly not conducive to effectively dealing with an incident. Furthermore, in the simulations as in the case of actual events, many of the exercises were timed to begin just before or during a shift change, thereby creating additional problems in not only providing necessary police for the area in and around the perimeter but also maintaining the capability to continue routine operations. This was especially difficult in smaller units that did not have the capacity to develop a surge capability of their own. Finally, such factors as heavy rainfall and freezing weather created difficulties for departments already facing organizational and behavioral stress.

The problem was further exacerbated as outside help arrived, even if a history of cooperation or formal memorandums of agreement to assist in critical incidents existed. In many cases, although the local county sheriff department and nearby jurisdictions had worked together, most did not have the necessary multijurisdictional training to deal with an act of terrorism, which is inherently multijurisdictional in nature. This difficulty became even more obvious when federal law enforcement arrived, often a while after the first responders and other local jurisdictions were in place. While these federal agencies were indeed ultimately responsible for dealing with an incident, the "I'm in charge here" syndrome creates additional tensions in an already pressurized situation. Bureaucratic battles should not take place during an incident. To a degree, this problem has been recognized in the multijurisdictional simulations that now take place, but as noted earlier, they are often too scripted, and all too often the local first responders are relegated to a support role when their knowledge of the area and their training could be put to far better use.

This bureaucratic multijurisdictional competition, in more than one instance, has hampered even the preparation of a simulation, as each agency or department wants to be involved in writing the script, or exercise plan (ExPlan), as a means of having an advantage and projecting a good image during an exercise. This problem is further compounded by the complexity of preparing simulations to meet the requirements of the Department of Homeland Security and the increased availability of a wide variety of tactical teams with very uneven training. Thus, at a time when the need for simplicity and unity of command is needed in both simulations and actual incidents, the law enforcement "community" often does not act as a unified entity. This is further magnified by the expanded role of the military in domestic law enforcement—especially in regard to terrorism. Finally, when there are numerous units on or near the impacted area, one can be certain that such activity will attract not only the traditional news media but also a new generation of "news hawks" with their hand-held cameras, thereby creating a problem of crowd control. Moreover, the ensuing coverage will in all probability generate fear in the community, which is a basic objective of the terrorists. There is a great deal to be learned from other countries such as the United Kingdom, where "low-visibility operations" are conducted by highly trained small specialized units secure in their authority to act decisively. But because ultimately "all terrorism is local," local police forces (individually and with others) must be involved in simulations to prepare them for an actual incident. This particularly applies to active-shooter scenarios where they will not have the luxury to wait for external help, since, as noted earlier, time is not on the side of the authorities.

OVERCOMMUNICATION AND THE "CNN SYNDROME"

The remarkable development of technology, especially in communication, has ironically acted both as an asset and as a liability in dealing with terrorist threats and incidents. In the early simulations, there were constant problems associated with what is now called crisis communication. First, radio/telephone discipline was often lacking, so limited radio frequencies were often overloaded; that led to a fundamental barrier in the development of vital command and control. Second, at the inception of simulated incidents little attention was given in many instances to having the necessary jacks and equipment (in the pre–mobile phone stage) for the initial on-site command post. Third, the constant use of mobile radios often led to a very serious technological failure: the radio batteries would be depleted, and a loss of communication would take place, often at the most crucial time of negotiation or in preparation for an assault. Finally, in the early exercises, the responding forces were not cognizant of the importance of communication security. All too often, the media, as well as the terrorists, got a blow-by-blow account of what the responding forces were doing through the use of commercially available police scanners. Indeed, in our exercises, the terrorists almost always had monitors as a means of anticipating the response of civilian police forces.

Technological advancements have greatly increased the variety of available means of communication. Ideally, such technology should enhance the capability of single or multiple forces to effectively communicate. But this availability can also lead to overcommunication, with everyone using cell phones without the necessary discipline. The problem is aggravated by the so-called CNN Syndrome, in which the images of an event are continually replayed without the addition of new information or without being placed in context, thereby further heightening public fear.[6] Moreover, the ready use of hand-held cameras and even camera-phones that can take high-quality pictures and videos makes securing the scene of an incident difficult. The ever-present Internet poses a particular problem, for, once the world of alternative media becomes active, a combination of misinformation and the product of sheer rumor or imagination can overstate a threat and spread public alarm. Future simulations will have to deal with these new developments because, however skillful, the authorities cannot possibly control all lines of communication. Even in countries where press blackouts are possible, the impact of alternative sources of communication makes controlling the information environment difficult.

In addition to overcommunication, responding forces now face another problem. Given the availability of databases and other forms of information that were not available in the early simulations and actual incidents, both the police or military forces and their intelligence units face the risk of being overwhelmed with information. We now have a plethora of databases, and half the problem of communication rests in effective information handling. Finally, as noted earlier, those involved in future simulations will have to deal with "virtual terrorism," in which an incident might not be actually taking place but the perpetrators, through their skillful use of the Internet and modern computer-generated and videotaped editing, can "create" an incident and alter the perception of the viewers concerning an imaginary threat so that it seems all too real.[7] Future simulations will have to address "The Wilderness of Mirrors," in which whatever is being presented on the television screen or the computer may be either real or falsified.

REACHING THE HIGHEST LEVEL

In the earliest simulations, when smaller local police forces responded, the police chief and his or her senior staff would be involved in both the preparation and the conduct of the simulations. This involvement was vital for two reasons. First, it indicated the commitment of the organization to carrying out the exercise. Second, those who would be the key decision makers in an actual incident would be directly involved in the training. However, with exercises in larger departments, it would at times be difficult to get the direct involvement of the senior officers, because the simulations were placed under the training command. Thus, one would not always get the necessary high-level support, and perhaps even more importantly, senior executives would not be involved in the exercise. This truncated chain of command, in which more-junior officers were used to conduct the exercise or serve as stand-ins for their superiors, detracted from the exercises. The most realistic simulations, as in the case of actual incidents, at some time may require the highest level of decision making, especially in a high-profile incident of terrorism.

There was no substitute for the level of support and the reality of the simulation in an exercise in Berlin, where the commanding general and his battle staff were directly involved in an exercise that lasted for almost twenty-four hours. The pressure to act correctly at 3:00 a.m. after being up for twenty hours was very real. But in virtually all of the exercises, there was a significant omission: key political leaders were not involved in the exercise. This was unfortunate, because in a major incident, how the civilian leadership will act is important. Will they have the will and training to understand and deal with a major incident? There has been marked improvement in this area.

In recent large-scale exercises, senior police and military officers as well as their civilian leadership and political leaders have been involved in exercises. This model adheres to the British experience, where the prime minister has been fully engaged. There is no substitute for having everyone from the beat cop to the major or the governor experiencing a realistic exercise. In this instance, the participation of the top of the hierarchy does matter. But with that, there also is a danger that political considerations, including competition among strong leaders of different agencies and departments and micromanagement, can act as an impediment to the effective use of forces that are trained to make the appropriate tactical (if not political) decisions. Identifying these political and bureaucratic fault lines in an exercise is far better than discovering them in the real thing.

WHAT MAKES ONE A CONVINCING TERRORIST

If a simulation is to provide the type of realistic training that will hopefully lessen the possibility that Murphy's Law will happen in a real situation, very careful selection and training of the terrorists and other lead players in an exercise must take place. Unfortunately, there tends to be a serious omission in the training: while there is a good chance that one could easily recruit tactically qualified red teams, neither the teams nor other participants may have the necessary acting skill to enhance their credibility so that the responding forces "suspend their disbelief" and accept that, for all intents and purposes, they are in an actual incident and not an exercise. In the early simulations, the problem of finding individuals who were tactically qualified and felt confident that they could both control the situation within the perimeter and meet the challenges created by the police or military forces was not difficult.

In several instances, Sloan used special forces personnel (and indeed, in one case, a crack counterterrorism unit in Germany) to be the red team. But in an especially protracted siege, skilled actors who could use their talent to enhance the reality of the situation were necessary. In some cases, this occurred; in others, the capacity to provide a demanding and realistic threat was diminished because of the lack of acting skills. In a couple of situations, individuals lacking both tactical and acting skills were introduced into the exercise without the knowledge or permission of the simulation director. Consequently, they neither provided a physical challenge to the police nor effectively portrayed terrorists. In one exercise (happily, not directed by either of the authors), a poorly trained community theater group took on the roles of not only acting as terrorists but also making tactical decisions. Because of their lack of experience and confidence in establishing control of the hostages, "the gang that could not shoot straight" used totally unnecessary force, as well as other forms of inappropriate behavior. In this instance, one of the deans of the university where this simulation took place was pushed to the floor and received a bloody nose—not a good way to start an exercise. Other faux pas in training, witnessed by Bunker, have included a terrorist operative getting into a fetal position and shutting down when the shooting started and an instance in which an untrained terrorist leader decided to advance though buildings far away from the objective and in the process got his cell members overly fatigued, lost, and separated from one another.

The problems associated with recruiting appropriate individuals have now been complicated by the need to acquire trained personnel who represent various ethnic groups, speak the language of the "terrorists," and have the cultural sensitivity and acculturation to fully get into their roles (see chapters 5 and 6). This selection process is vital for believability and is a central element of a good simulation.

THE COMMUNITY AS A KEY PLAYER

Because terrorism is not solely aimed at individuals but targets a broader community, involving the community in simulations is important. Unfortunately, this was not the case in most of the early exercises, which were essentially limited to uniformed and civilian members of the governmental sector. An act of terrorism, as Brian Jenkins noted, is "aimed at the people watching"; how they respond individually and collectively may be significant not only at the start of an incident but also during the event and after it is over.[8] Even if an incident is being handled properly, if the public does not know or understand what is taking place, they may react to the images they see. Context, again, is vital.

Therefore, the public as stakeholders in facing terrorism should be involved in simulations. Key opinion makers, clergy, and other formal and informal leaders, through their involvement, can act as knowledgeable sources of information if an attack occurs. In smaller communities especially, the word of respected and well-known individuals may have more credibility than that of a state or national spokesperson. There have certainly been very impressive accounts of having the help of the public in major incidents. The response of the citizens of Oklahoma, the surrounding area, and the nation to the bombing of the Federal Building, for example, was quite impressive. There was the view that "we are all in this together"; such an attitude not only provided an impressive amount of material and physical support for the responders but also helped to start to heal the trauma of the event. Certainly, the response by the public to the 9/11 attacks in New York and Washington, D.C., was equally impressive. In events of such a magnitude, civil defense, now known as community emergency response, could have proven helpful. One wonders whether, had smaller communities addressed potential threats such as school shootings or terrorism in advance and experienced realistic but not overthreatening exercises, such incidents even when not prevented would have generated less hysteria. In effect, simulations should be part of an integrated program of terrorism education on the state, local, and national level.

THE NEED FOR FLEXIBILITY AND RESILIENCE

Given the uncertainty, complexity, and dynamics of any terrorist incident, even with the best training Murphy's Law will still occur. With the benefit of hindsight, it is all too easy to recognize errors that led to a botched rescue attempt or the failed apprehension of perpetrators before they engaged in a killing spree, be it at a school or at a military installation. After-action reports are filled with "lessons that can be learned" from such defects in counterterrorism responses. But one must always remember that those who are involved in a critical situation do not have the luxury of hindsight in a supercharged environment; they will have to act, and how they act will help determine the outcome. Given this consideration, whether the errors consist of a breakdown in communication, a failure of technology, or a bureaucratic battle within or among responding forces, one thing is clear: no matter the level of training, there is no substitute for effective leadership, disciplined and trained forces, and, perhaps most important, the ability of all those involved in a simulation or training exercise to adjust and make rapid decisions in the face of the constant changes that accompany an act of terrorism.

CHAPTER 5

THE RED TEAM

Developing an Adversarial Perspective

For the first few days, Matt and I were the only red team trainees to wear our kaffiyeh and continually eat traditional Arab meals to get into the proper role.

—Robert Bunker, 2004

The mission of the red team is to provide a thinking and sentient enemy (or opposing force) that will appropriately challenge the good guys undergoing the terrorist simulation and make them reevaluate and/or develop their tactics, response protocols, and counterterrorism doctrine. Law enforcement officers are typically used to the behaviors of common criminals who will attempt to flee when confronted, are reactionary in their behaviors, and will resort to force only—even then in only some instances—when they are cornered or trapped. The red team is meant to mimic the actions of an operative, a cell, or a larger element within an opposing terrorist organization. Unlike common criminals, terrorists operate under a whole different mindset and are far more proactive and military-like in their behaviors.[1] The most recent national experiences with somewhat similar behaviors can be seen with the North Hollywood shootout in 1997, the Columbine High School massacre in 1999, and the Beltway sniper attacks of 2002. Still, from a red teaming perspective, these would be considered the actions of second-string terrorists at best. The other extreme—with 9/11 being the current pinnacle of achievement—is evident with the operations of far more sophisticated groups such as Al Qaeda,

Hezbollah, and Chechen insurgents. Red teaming itself is more of an art than a science, and gaining an adversarial perspective requires not only mimicking the behaviors of a terrorist group or lone operative but also understanding the capabilities that they do and do not possess and their intent and motivations. Knowledge of terrorist doctrine, past incident patterns and group signatures, and ideology are thus essential, as is extensive tactical experience. In developing an adversarial perspective, the following guidelines apply.

RED TEAM MEMBERS MUST TRY TO "FEEL AND THINK" LIKE TERRORISTS

Gaining "terrorist insights and instinct" is a critical requirement for red team personnel. The biggest obstacle to getting into a terrorist mindset for many red team members consists of one's beliefs, personal biases, and love of country. Terrorists are vehemently disliked and loathed by military and law enforcement personnel, with "kinetic solutions" being the preferred method for dealing with them. For this reason—essentially, one of cognitive dissonance—active-duty law enforcement and military personnel do not normally make the best red team members. To tell a Marine with the institutional memory of the 1983 Beirut Barracks bombing in his heart or a New York City police officer who lost comrades in 2001 at the World Trade Center that they are going to not only take on the roles of "Islamic freedom fighters" but also see the world from that cultural perspective is extremely difficult if not impossible. One method to contend with this problem is through "terrorist immersion training," which the Mirror Image course offered by the Terrorism Research Center (TRC) essentially is. This unique course created in 2002 is "an intensive, one-week classroom and field training program, designed to realistically simulate terrorist recruiting, training techniques and operational tactics."[2] Multiple daily

prayer sessions, a steady diet of Middle Eastern cuisine, weapons and tactical training, and bonding time with your terrorist
cellmates helps to make for a lasting impression. The course is
only offered to U.S. law enforcement, military, government, and
other specially vetted personnel. Still, it is an uphill struggle to
culturally indoctrinate some of the trainees:

> This baptism into militant Islam proved tough for some.
> A young Army officer seated next to me, who'd recently
> returned from Iraq, developed a severe twitch in his jaw
> muscles as Navid went on to claim that Christians are
> backward polytheists who may legitimately be killed
> under Koranic law. As we rose for break, the officer swore,
> "These people are all so two-faced. They talk about reli-
> gion, but show me an Iraqi who doesn't chain-smoke and
> drink."
>
> "It almost makes me sick listening to their bullshit,"
> agreed a Secret Service agent.[3]

Another approach to the lack of cultural and ideological
empathy is the training now provided by the U.S. Army's University of Foreign Military and Cultural Studies (UFMCS) at
Fort Leavenworth, Kansas. That group began offering a comprehensive eighteen-week Red Team Leader's Course in 2006
that draws heavily upon anthropology and regional studies
in addition to unconventional military theory, doctrine, and
historical instances of red teaming. Shorter, more specialized
red teaming courses are now also being offered by UFMCS.
The intent is to create course graduates with more-refined critical thinking skills and to develop alternative points of view
for army battle staffs deployed overseas in such theaters as
Iraq and Afghanistan. One component of this enculturation
process is the use of movie nights that portray Middle Eastern documentaries and such celebrated counterinsurgency
films as *The Battle of Algiers*.[4] That same film was shown to a

law enforcement audience a few years earlier (in 2002) in Garden Grove, California, at a counterterrorism institute Bunker helped to coordinate. Documentaries, films, and online propaganda and recruitment videos created by terrorist and insurgent groups provide a wonderful means to gain insights into the terrorist mindset. Particular attention should also be paid to the dress, customs, mannerisms, and personal habits of the subjects in the films and videos. Some cultures, for example, will sit cross-legged at war councils and tactical deliberations, while others may squat, kneel, stand, or use chairs.

To forestall the development of "cultural threat myopia" and to allow for other threat groups to be simulated, red team members should be exposed to other terrorist perspectives. One should not forget that the Oklahoma City bombing (1995) and the Centennial Park bombing (1996) were carried out by white supremacists and an antiabortionist, respectively, who were former U.S. Army personnel with either infantry combat or explosive training. To better appreciate white supremacist thinking, red teams should read such tomes as *The Turner Diaries* and *The Hunter,* along with literature providing a basic understanding of concerns relating to the Zionist Occupation Government (ZOG) and the incidents in Waco, Texas, with the Branch Davidians and at Ruby Ridge, Idaho, with the Weaver family. A violent antiabortionist mindset can be better understood through the study of Army of God (AOG) writings and works such as *Vigilantes of Christendom: The Story of the Phineas Priesthood* and by reviewing affiliated extremist Web sites with the appropriate anonymizer for one's computer browser.

OUTSIDERS TO THE GROUP BEING TRAINED SHOULD BE USED AS RED TEAM MEMBERS

In many of the original exercises conducted by Sloan among the police and the military groups, detailed in *Simulating Terrorism,* personnel from the same profession or units as those of the blue team and other participants played the role of the terrorists. The outcomes were often flawed because the terrorists spoke the same language and shared many values with the very hostages they "captured" or with the police they were engaging. Moreover, many of them actually had to return to duty and work with the very hostages they had "captured" or with the same police they had challenged. In such cases, participants in the exercise may lack the perspective necessary if the supposed terrorists are to test the capacity of the responding forces effectively. This resulted in a conscious policy of not selecting individuals to play the roles of terrorists in the simulations who are members of the police forces or who have extensive law enforcement experience.

Because, in real life, terrorists reject the society in which they find themselves (particularly the forces of law and order), they do not share the values of the forces they are marshaled against. Therefore, in a simulation, the terrorists should not come from the very organizations they are to attack. In preparation for the simulation, the terrorists must turn their backs on the social order because they are to play outsiders who cannot be part of it: they are not members of the governmental, law enforcement, or military community. If personnel from any of these communities have to be used as red team members—and this should kept to a bare minimum—those with educational backgrounds in anthropology or foreign studies or who have grown up in the non-Western world, as well as those who have served as undercover officers, intelligence operatives, or foreign area officers (FAOs) or have been in Special Operations Forces (SOF), are preferred.

In rare cases, military personnel have been successfully utilized for counterterrorism red teaming; the famed Red Cell, a classified U.S. Navy counterterrorist group drawn from SEAL Team Six members in the mid-1980s, comes to mind. That group was used in the penetration of U.S. naval bases worldwide for simulated terrorist destruction of facilities and materiel, assassination, and hostage-taking purposes, with the operations being video-taped for training purposes. The program was highly successful because of the "outlaw" and "anything goes" perspective of the team members but ultimately created bureaucratic and political fallout. The Red Cell program was shut down in 1992, but most of its field activities had been curtailed years earlier.[5]

A "TRAIN AS YOU FIGHT, FIGHT AS YOU TRAIN" PHILOSOPHY MUST BE FOLLOWED

Bad habits, training shortcuts, and inappropriate muscle memories (such as wrong finger placement by the trigger) exhibited by red team members are generally unprofessional and detrimental to the simulation. Not only do they shortchange the training of the participants, and potentially imperil them during real missions, but also lax standards and bad habits can readily carry over to real-world situations in which red team members may find themselves. However, a caveat must be added to these perceptions: if amateur terrorists or individuals engaging in terrorist-like behaviors, such as teen active shooters, are being red teamed, they may or not be sloppy and unprofessional in their tactical approach. A debate over teen active-shooter tactical skill proficiency exists, however, with Dave Grossman asserting that video games have become "mass murder simulators" and "marksmanship trainers" that have made the shooters more proficient with firearms, in some instances, than the responding police forces are.[6]

Red team members, once in bad-guy character and in tactical mode, must approach the simulation as a real-life incident. In prolonged simulations, red team members do not subscribe to a 9–5 workday and will skimp on meals and sleep as necessary to fulfill the operation. Western ideals of chivalry and any notions of fair play also quickly become foreign concepts for the red team. Bunker was in a simulation in which the Gaza cell—his cell—was given the objective of capturing and abducting a VIP from a guarded facility. The squad-size cell had at its disposal several pistols and assault weapons, a suicide bomber rig, and a couple of cars. Additionally, during that scenario, a real life CNN TV crew was covering the exercise for a story it was doing on counterterrorism training. Not to be daunted by their limited resources, the Gaza cell members improvised, as all well-trained terrorists do to help further the success of their operation, with two cunning ploys. The first ploy focused on the CNN cameraman. He was recruited to the cause and made to wear the suicide bomber rig as part of the first phase of the assault plan. The precedent for such an attack can be found with the assassination of Ahmad Shah Massoud ("Lion of Panjshir") on September 10, 2001, by two Arab suicide bombers posing as a TV news crew. As the two exercise cars with some of the Gaza team members headed toward the front of the targeted facility, the cameraman detonated his rig next to the defending guards, taking them out of the scenario. The second ploy involved the motor pool. Just prior to the launch of the operation, additional vehicles were requisitioned; these included a couple of nice rental cars and a beat-up facility car parked nearby with the keys in the ignition. The remaining defending forces were totally surprised by the additional cars that showed up during the second phase of the assault, allowing for the main Gaza cell team to quickly dismount and make an entry through the rear door of the facility to secure their objective.

A "train as you fight, fight as you train" philosophy must thus be followed, with team members giving it their all. This can be especially difficult to do on hot days when heavy protective gear is being worn or when lack of proper gear, such as gloves for the hands or arm padding, results in the accumulation of minor injuries such as skin missing from the impact of sim-rounds or getting bruised from going over obstacles. If proper safety protocols are followed and participants stay hydrated and are allowed cool-down periods, medical concerns are typically a nonissue. Ultimately, if the red team members take both their roles and the simulation seriously and are dedicated to providing the best training that they can, a transformation will take place. As the individual terrorists assume their identities and develop a collective consciousness, the preparation for the planned assault should transform each of them from a person playacting as a terrorist to a terrorist preparing to initiate an operation in which, for the duration of the simulation, he believes and to which he is committed even if the outcome ends in "bloodshed." It is thus that an emotional stage is set for the physical attack.

For Matt Begert, a current Mirror Image cell leader, this emotional divide was crossed during the leading of his terrorist cell on an assault against a scenario objective. He was moving forward, and out of the corner of his eye he caught a glimpse of a figure moving on his flank. His tactical instincts took over, and without hesitation he shot up the threat with multiple sim-rounds from his Glock pistol, neutralizing the individual. After the scenario was over, the targeted individual, who happened to be an observer who had strayed too close to Matt and his red team, complained about being targeted. Matt's reply was simply that he was a terrorist engaging in a mission and that the individual, considered an immediate threat, was eliminated. There are no limitations or restrictions on terrorists, such as would be faced by a police officer. The objective is to attack and kill.[7]

For Bunker, this same feeling hit him as he was assaulting forward into a classroom during a tactical simulation. The author was quickly moving in support of the other red team member, who had taken position in the back of the classroom and was being engaged by a responding police tactical unit who had made entry. By the front classroom doorway were two motionless bodies of individuals who in that scenario had earlier been shot by the active shooters. The intent of the assault was to surprise the police officers from the rear and have

Bunker making a tactical assault into a high school classroom over fallen shooting victims. A Claremont Police contact team had just entered the classroom to engage one active shooter and was being hit from behind by another one. Courtesy of Gabriel Fenoy, *The Claremont Courier.*

the trainers engage them from both the front and the back simultaneously. Note that the orientation of the gun in Bunker's hand in the picture is slightly pointed downward, when it should have been held level and directed forward. The reason for this positioning is that a second or two earlier, he had actually contemplated putting a quick round into the head of each of the shooting victims to ensure an execution-style kill and, in essence, making an overt "political statement" to the police that this is a fight to the death.

EACH SIMULATION WILL REQUIRE THE GENERATION OF A NEW RED TEAM

The creation of a red team is determined by identifying the actual terrorist group or type of terrorist threat that will represent the opposing force and by conceptualizing the type of terrorist simulation (active aggressor, hostage taking, or intelligence driven) that will be taking place. The red team will have a mission within the context of the simulation, and the actual carrying out of this mission will be determined by the intent, capability, dedication, and cultural/religious characteristics of the simulated terrorist force. Before recruitment or selection of the "terrorists," it is thus necessary to create the program and related ideology that the assaulting group would use to justify their actions (and demands if applicable). In most of the original *Simulating Terrorism* simulations, the ideological makeup of the terrorist group was a mixture of left-wing rhetoric and anarchistic positions. The declarations of the group usually consisted of provocative statements relating to the destruction of the establishment and a call for revolutionary action. The international ties of the terrorist group were continually stressed in statements that the organization was part of a movement that included highly publicized groups, such as the United Red Army and the Red Brigades. The call for action was primarily in terms of exhorting "the masses" to domestic violence. The implication was constantly made that the terrorists were part of a larger transnational coalition, thereby indicating that the incident was not simply a local problem.

International and domestic relations and, along with them, terrorist threats have drastically changed. Active-aggressor red teams can now be modeled on a continuum from one or two teen active shooters carrying pistols and rifles and ideologically fueled by nihilism and rage all the way to multiple fundamentalist Islamic terrorist operational cells utilizing assault weapons, suicide backpacks, rocket-propelled grenades (RPGs), and body armor for protection. The possibility of sniper and countersniper deployments and the use of car bombs as active assault components or as secondary devices along avenues of approach to kill responding forces now also exist. One example of a highly coordinated active-aggressor incident is found in Riyadh with the multiple Al Qaeda attacks and penetrations of the U.S.- and other foreign-worker compounds in May 2003. Mexican drug cartel tactical units composed of former Mexican special forces personnel represent another potential red team to be simulated. This fact became evident with the assassination of a drug dealer in Phoenix in June 2008 by a cartel hit team whose members were dressed and outfitted to look like Phoenix Police Department SWAT officers. An even more ominous fact was that the cartel team had a contingency plan to ambush any pursuing police officers during their "escape and evasion" from the scene of the assassination in a nearby alley. Luckily, the lone Phoenix tactical officer who initially responded to the incident sensed an ambush, established a perimeter, and waited until more reinforcements arrived before engaging the drug cartel operatives and helping to arrest them.[8] The ballads of the narcotraffickers, their spiritual admiration for Jesus Malverde and Santa Muerte, and the torture and beheading methods of the cartels and their enforcers, along with their more traditional tactics and doctrine, will all become necessary knowledge for red teams to properly simulate this emergent threat.

Hostage taking based on the late 1960s and 1970s model has not fully disappeared but is now the exception rather than the norm of today's, and quite probably tomorrow's, terrorist operations. The archetypes of this form of operation are the assorted aerial hijackings of the era and the Munich Massacre of 1972, though the later U.S. Embassy takeover in Tehran from 1979 through 1981 and the *Achille Lauro* cruise ship hijacking of 1985 fall within the original hostage-taking pattern. Trends since the 1990s, however, suggest that, when hostage taking now occurs, more extreme levels of violence will ensue. This evolution from "symbolic violence and a stage play" to a willingness to engage in mass killing with little substantive negotiation can be seen with the Chechen takeovers of the Kizlyar-Pervomayskoye hospital and village in 1996, the Dubrovka Theater in Moscow in 2002, and the Beslan School in 2004, and Al Qaeda's use of commercial jetliners (full of hostages) as flying suicide-bombing vehicles in 2001. Where modern hostage taking may more closely represent older patterns is with legacy and secular terrorist groups devoid of a dominant religious ideology and narco-criminal entities that are engaging in hostage taking for ransom or for limited political purposes such as to engage in prisoner exchanges.

Intelligence-driven simulations are a high priority these days with the continued threat and specter of terrorist WMD use. The most recent instances of this threat can be seen with the anthrax letters of late 2001 in the United States, the use of chlorine bombs in Iraq in 2006–2007, and the suspected deaths of forty Al Qaeda members in Algeria in early 2009 from the plague (Black Death). Threat groups in this regard are predominantly radical Islamic, with Al Qaeda and affiliates topping the list, followed currently by white supremacy adherents. However, groups such as Al Qaeda and those belonging to the Creativity movements (Church of the Creator decedents) have vastly different cultural and symbolic perspectives in their use of terrorism; therefore, Creativity employment of WMD might utilize some form of rational targeting basis, for example, directed at synagogues or ethnic churches, whereas Al Qaeda's WMD use might make no rational targeting sense to us because the target of the attack may be important only for the radical group or its constituent audiences.[9]

RED TEAM MEMBERS SHOULD BE RECRUITED IN NUMBERS AND DIVERSITY TO FULFILL THE NEEDS OF THE SIMULATION

While one of the principal tenets of military operations is "economy of force," the other extreme also applies, that is, having not merely the minimum number of personnel needed to do the mission but also some sort of reserve force. In the creation of a red team, the number of members should be balanced and weighted by the size, requirements, and duration of the simulation. At the low end, a couple of red team members will suffice for active-shooter training where the simulation is focused on one or two opposing force members engaging in school, workplace, or public venue violence. Midrange requirements are based on simulating the needs of a small tactical cell of terrorists ranging from five to eight members. Upper-range requirements would involve simulating multiple terrorist tactical cells working together, which would result in ten or more red team members being required. Having a few extra red team members to cycle through the simulation may be prudent in case of injury or exhaustion from physical assertion. For the needs of some simulations—such as active surveillance and the penetration of a targeted facility for information gathering and reconnaissance purposes—extra red team personnel are essential to replace operatives as they get "burned" (potentially identified by guards or countersurveillance forces) or use up their loiter time on or near the target prior to being considered potential opposing force threats.

The mixture of backgrounds, professions, and skill sets for those participants used to populate the red team force should then be considered. For active-shooter simulations, tactical firearms experience and physical fitness are two of the most important considerations for red team members. Suicide-bomber simulations do not necessarily have the same red team requirements, as suicide bombers are typically neither experienced with firearms nor physically fit—they just have to be willing to strap a bomb to themselves or drive a vehicle full of explosives and blow themselves up. Even the bomber handlers do not require too much expertise—possibly a basic understanding of countersurveillance and operational security measures, but that is pretty minimal. If a security element is present, then active-shooter member requirements can be followed. Because protective headgear will be worn over the head and face, age and ethnicity considerations do not generally come into play for the above active-aggressor simulations. Still, getting the responding forces used to engaging women, minorities, and different ages, especially teenagers, as opponents has its merits. As discussed earlier, red team members should not come from the actual organization being trained or its culture, such as having police training other police. Ideally, red team members who have reviewed terrorist tactical methods (or, even better, have actual training in them) would be preferred, but such individuals are still somewhat elusive to find.

For hostage simulations, drawing upon former terrorists as advisors, upon those who have interviewed them in the field (news reporters) or in prison (intelligence officers and some scholars), and upon those who have profiled terrorists or have done in-depth studies on their psychology and past operations would be ideal. Individuals such as these are very rare commodities, however; if access to them is possible, they should be utilized to their fullest. For most organizations and groups, works such as this (and those listed in the bibliography) may for some time provide the best initial simulation guidance. Minorities, the old, the young, and women can all have integral parts to play as red team members in hostage, as well as intelligence-driven, simulations. The original *Simulating Terrorism* work discusses how the organization takes on further identity when women and various minority groups are deliberately recruited. This recruitment is meant in part to reflect the multiethnic composition that has been noted on occasion in terrorist groups. It also creates an interesting diversity of outlook among the organization's members, who must develop cohesiveness for the impending simulation. The selection of different nationality groups and women is meant primarily to create crucial problems in human relationships, which must be handled by the responding forces, particularly by the hostage negotiators, during the conduct of the simulation.

A particular example of the utility of using older persons in a simulation was noted during relatively recent countersurveillance training that Bunker participated in. In the training, hostile surveillance was being conducted on multiple public venues in the urban center of a medium-sized American city. (The reason was not provided, but similar surveillance would be done for stand-up assault, hostage taking, or bombing purposes.) The author, who coordinated the countersurveillance force at one of the venues, like his team members was initially expecting to be up against undercover intelligence officers or at least sworn-duty personnel. Police officer profiles of well-groomed men in their thirties and forties with small mustaches came to mind for criminal intelligence officers, while the undercover officers might be slightly younger men with tattoos, jeans, and hooded jerseys or some other edgy blue-collar attribute. Instead, they were up against a mixture of older police reservists—some of whom had to be in their late sixties and early seventies—from both sexes and with a variety of ethnic groupings thrown in. The author's team pretty quickly recovered from this initial and potentially deadly profiling error in the course of the daylong field exercise. It even had its own successes in deploying older people as its main street operatives. One team member was an older African American male who was dressed up as a security guard in front of a building in the vicinity of the targeted venue, which allowed him fixed loiter time for surveillance purposes. Another team member, an older white woman, who had a PhD in psychology, removed all makeup, dirtied herself, put on stained bag-lady clothes, and utilized a walker as a prop. She represented a mobile surveillance force (with loiter capability) and was so masterful in her role that at one point one of the "burned" surveillance team members took pity on her and helped her across the street. The lesson learned, of course, is that using people other than adult white males in the simulations provides new perspectives and capabilities that heretofore did not exist. Also, because the terrorists themselves often do not fit the adult white male profile, making the simulation as realistic as possible by accurately modeling the age, sex, and ethnicity demographic of the opposing threat group further helps to maximize its realism.

Some additional thoughts should be considered concerning terrorists and specialized skill sets with regard to hostage simulations. Terrorist group leadership emerges from individuals who are conversant with the rhetoric of radical politics or have the ability to write effectively. For example, in one of the original exercises, one of the rhetoricians was a professional writer whose best-selling novels included plots associated with terrorist incidents. The specialized skills of the recruits can be utilized especially well when the target is a high-technology installation. In the seizure of an oil refinery, for example, a petroleum engineer was recruited into the band so that his skills could be utilized against the plant. Despite this specialization of function, all the terrorists (just as in actual hostage-taking incidents) should be trained in rudimentary weapons handling, seizing hostages, and other essential military skills that must be employed in a successful operation. As in any actual small-size operation, terrorists cannot afford the luxury of separating the staff functions from the line functions. The absence of specialization is one way that they differ from the responding forces.

Concerning intelligence-driven simulations, most of the red team member requirements for hostage simulations are in effect, with a few caveats. First, scientific and technical skills become extremely important, given the nature of chemical, biological, radiological, and nuclear (CBRN) weapons and dispersal devices. One or more members of the opposing force team should possess some form of technical skills and knowledge pertaining to the weapon to be utilized in the simulation. They would take on the role of the WMD maker. If this is impossible, then such an individual should be consulted concerning the precursor agents and substances, manufacture, handling, and operational use of the scenario weapon in the creation of the exercise. Scientific accuracy is all-important in these forms of simulations; however, scientists are typically nonoperational in their thinking. As a result, weaponization and actual deployment problems (as was seen in the Tokyo subway sarin gas attack in 1995) readily take place. Such problems need to be thought out, as do issues of weather conditions and urban microclimates and whether other subject-matter expertise is required in that regard. Because these simulations are intelligence-driven—rather than active-shooter, hostage, or render-safe response, though they can certainly contain such scenarios within them—red team members with a broader knowledge of terrorist attack cycles and the use of deception in operations are more useful than those with primarily tactical skills. In one exercise, Bunker was running both a strategic and operational "factual inject" and "deception inject" master scenario events list (MSEL) for a biological attack against a subway system many weeks ahead of the actual exercise. The intent is for those being trained to sharpen their analytical skills pertaining to pattern and anomaly analysis of red team activity.

DETERMINATION OF THE APPROPRIATE LEVEL OF RED TEAM ACTIVITIES MUST BE MADE

When the red team goes up against the forces being trained in the simulation, the red team members must continually monitor not only themselves but also the actions of their team in relationship to the actions of the good guys, because the intent of the training is to appropriately challenge law enforcement, responder, and potentially even military personnel and to better hone their individual and unit counterterrorism skills. Referees and simulation monitors are great resources in this regard and can be talked with offline between scenarios or during lull points within the context of a larger scenario taking place. Only through ongoing feedback and checks to monitor the training can the best simulation experience be provided.

The question becomes, What is appropriate counterterrorism training for those being trained in the simulation? This determination initially was made when the simulation was created and took in various factors related to the intent of the simulation; the makeup of the red team and the threat to be used in the development of the scenario; and the expertise, sophistication, and training state of the individuals and units being trained. As the actual training is being conducted, this "initial intent" will be modified as required to fine-tune the training, hence the value of unscripted or minimally scripted play. Nothing is more disastrous or wastes more training time than scripted or canned play that is too far below the training and sophistication level of the trainees or too far above their present capabilities and skill sets. Possibly the only insult that can be added to such injury is to utilize red team members and trainers who have little expertise in the subject matter and are, in essence, "bright-eyed and bushy-tailed" script monkeys.

To appropriately challenge the good guys below zone, in zone, and above zone, red team activities used against the forces being trained must be well thought-out, properly implemented, and continually fine-tuned. The majority of the training should be in zone for the forces being trained, that is, not too basic for them and not too advanced for them. With enough training time and multiple scenarios, the intensity and difficulty of the training can be increased as the trainees gain in confidence, unit cohesion, and skill sets. If only one scenario is being implemented in the simulation, then, as the scenario advances, more difficult injects can always be provided at the discretion of the referees, monitors, and trainers.

The easiest training is based on using amateur and non-preplanning active shooter and terrorist forces.[10] Wannabe terrorists are often found among groups including the mentally ill and emotionally unstable. Simulating these groups can also make for good initial training fodder. Such groups and individuals would typically fall into below-zone training because their tactical and operational decision-making process is erratic, irrational, and last minute in nature. In-zone training for many responding groups would be for them to go against simulated

"B-team" adversaries—bad guys with some military or military-like training. Such adversaries have done their homework, some basic surveillance and recon of their target, and have some sort of mission that they are implementing—for example, the killing of popular students at a high school, the taking of hostages for political purposes so that their grievances against the authorities can be aired or agendas furthered, or the detonation of a homemade weapon of mass destruction (such as an IED encased within radioactive medical waste) at an ethnic gathering. The vast majority of terrorist acts are probably committed by this level of adversary. Even more-advanced groups, such as Al Qaeda, now have mostly less-sophisticated affinity cells operating as part of their extended network. From this perspective, both the Madrid bombings of 2004 and the London bombings of 2005 would be considered the actions of B-team terrorists.

More-advanced and typically above-zone training would simulate the "A-team" adversaries. These terrorists are drawn from varying combinations of battle-hardened insurgents, former combat arms military and special forces personnel, talented businessmen and professionals, and highly trained and educated individuals with graduate and advanced degrees such as MDs and PhDs. The great danger with these adversaries is their analytical and preplanning skills, access to resources, great patience, ruthlessness, dedication to their cause, and understanding of not only military operations and tactics but also revolutionary warfare, insurgency, and terrorism to further their broader political, religious, and criminal agendas. While these adversaries can and do make mistakes, and may not always exhibit all the above skill sets and capabilities, they are the most dangerous opponents that U.S. law enforcement, responders, and the military presently have the potential to face. Familiar terrorists and groups that fall into this category would include Theodore Kaczynski, Ramiz Yousef, Timothy McVeigh, Mohamed Atta, Al Qaeda, Hezbollah, the Chechen insurgents, and Los Zetas.

CHAPTER 6

GETTING THE RED TEAM
READY FOR ITS ROLE

ROBERTA SLOAN, PhD

"Speak the speech, I pray you. . . . Let your own discretion be your tutor. Suit the action to the word, the word to the action. . . . Hold, as 'twere, the mirror up to nature."
—William Shakespeare, *Hamlet*

Many excellent ideas for getting the red team ready for its role are suggested in chapter 5: mimicking the behaviors of a terrorist group or a lone operative; understanding the capabilities that they do and do not possess; analyzing their intent and motivations; acquiring a knowledge of terrorist doctrine, past incident patterns, and group signatures and ideology. But helping red team members get ready for their roles goes beyond the activities suggested in the previous chapter, designed to assist in an enculturation process of the red team members.

It is certainly true, as previously suggested, that red teaming is more of an art than a science. To be effective, the red team members must actually try to feel and think like the terrorists, taking the transformative steps that are necessary to "become" their characters convincingly and to develop the necessary skills to work as a convincing team.

HOW THE RED TEAM MEMBER
APPROACHES THE ROLE

To become a convincing member of the red team, an individual team member must approach his or her particular terrorist character as an actor would approach preparing for a role to be played on the stage. The insightful suggestions in chapter 5 certainly lay a foundation for the group to approach their roles together, but each member of the team must also work on creating an individual character. This will preclude the common pitfall of "generalizing" a role, rather than developing the specific characteristics that will make the portrayal seem real. Each individual team member must therefore create a character.

Creating a Character

Regardless of whether your character figures prominently as a leader of the red team or becomes a more minor player in the scenario, the preparation must be intensive and complete. The vitality of the whole is made up of its parts. One person standing "out of character" or failing to concentrate in the right direction can lessen the effectiveness and believability of the entire team.

Prior to the actual simulation, keep your eyes open for people who you feel look and behave like the character you will be portraying. You might look for pictures in magazines and newspapers of people who, because of dress or circumstances, will help you create your part. Clip these pictures and begin a file dedicated to building your character. When ideas about your character occur to you, jot them down in your file. If you conduct anthropological or area research via the Internet or other sources, include copies of the information in your file. When you answer the questions posed later in this chapter, add those answers to your file. Ultimately, you will have a character file that will assist you in "becoming" your character within the context of the red team simulation.

Observing Other People Will Help You Develop Your Character

Observe the posture of other people. Choose a posture that you think might be indicative of the terrorist you will be playing. Make this posture distinct. Practice this posture when you are alone or in public places where people will not know you. Let the posture help you "get into the body" of your character.

Observe the expressions and gestures of other people. You do not have to choose just one person who you think might be similar to the character you are playing. Instead, you might choose to imitate one person's hand gestures, another person's facial expressions, and another person's walk. Virtually every living person indicates something of what is going on inside himself or herself through outward manifestations.

Observe the quotidian actions of other people. How one person walks, stands, sits, and eats, and even the size of his or her space bubble (that length of distance at which we position ourselves in the proximity of another person) can be very revealing.

These observations and your decision about which ones might work best for your role will help you delineate with specificity the personality of the character you will be playing. The decisions you make about these factors will have great impact on how you play your role. In other words, to prepare an amalgamation of characteristics that your character can use, you must observe others closely.

The Character Analysis

A character analysis of the terrorist you will be portraying, specific rather than general in nature, is important so that you will be convincing in your role. The following are some questions that you should ask yourself and decide about your character. There are no "right" or "wrong" answers. As long as your answers work within the larger context of the specific red team simulation as it has been explained to you, and they are consistent within the world of your character, your answers will help you to effectively build your role.

What are my character's physical traits? Decisions must be made as to sex, age, size, posture, rhythm, gait, gestures, and appearance.

What are my character's social traits? Decisions must be made as to class, profession, religion, economic status, family relationships, friendships, and habitual behaviors.

What are my character's psychological and moral traits? Decisions must be made as to your character's philosophy, value system, habits of thought, attitudes, desires, motivation, likes, dislikes, and the "eyes" through which you view the world.

What are my character's intentions/actions/obstacles? Decisions must be made as to your character's intentions, obstacles standing in the way of the intended goals, how your character attempts to fulfill the intentions, and to what lengths your character might go to achieve the intended goals.

What are my character's personal characteristics (as compared to my natural characteristics)? Decisions must be made as to how you are like or unlike your character and what personal experiences you can use to help you identify with the character you have chosen to play.

To make certain that you are totally familiar with your terror-ist character and that the character you portray is completely convincing, the following are some specific questions that you might ask yourself and decide about your character:

How old am I?

Where was I raised and educated?

What were the social and economic conditions of my family?

Am I married, and do I have children?

What might I habitually carry with me? Might it be a weapon, a good-luck charm, worry beads, and/or an insignia of my religion in the form of a piece of jewelry?

What are my hobbies, pastimes, and recreations? Do I play soccer? Do I read my holy book (or books)? Do I like to watch movies? Do I have a television?

What work do I do to support myself (and my family, if I have one)?

How much does my character hide or reveal about myself? Am I open or closed in conversation? Do I lie or tell the truth? If both, when do I do either, and in what context?

What is my training? Is it military/police/paramilitary?

What is my knowledge of weapons and tactics? Where did I learn them and from whom?

How committed am I to my cause? Would I die fighting or surrender? Am I being paid as a mercenary, or is this a cause that is essential to my self-image and belief system?

Have I served prison time? If so, for how long and where? For what was I incarcerated?

Am I mentally stable?

Am I currently using drugs for the mission? If so, how does that affect my behavior? Have I ever used drugs in the past?

What is my religion, and how devout am I? If I am devout, is this a way of life I grew up with, or did I adopt it in later years and under the influence of people I respected?

Has my upbringing, my training, or influences on me caused me to develop a cultural hatred toward another group of people?

What is my native language? Do I use key phrases or words, either in English or in my native tongue? (If it is possible for you to learn them, do so, and try to practice using them.)

What are some of the items indicative of my culture? Do I use perfumes or body oils? What do I eat? Does my breath normally smell of ethnic foods? Does this keep me from getting near other people or is nearness, despite smells, indicative of my cultural upbringing?

What are the mores within my culture with which I should be familiar? Do I stand close or far apart? Is the use of certain hand gestures considered forbidden or at the very least improper? Am I self-contained or effusive? Do I interrupt others or listen while they are speaking? Do I speak loudly or softly?

These are just some of the questions that you might answer in building your character. Taking the time to observe others, think about your character, and answer these questions in the context of the red team's simulation circumstances will help you develop a specific character that is believable within the "world" of the simulation.

IMPROVISATION TECHNIQUES THAT BUILD A CONVINCING RED TEAM

In chapter 5, it was suggested that unscripted or minimally scripted scenarios are far superior in simulations than

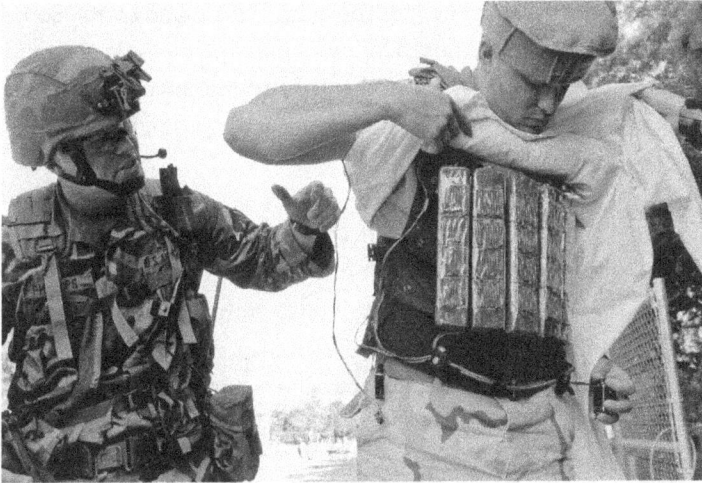

Training conducted with simulated suicide bombers is becoming increasingly frequent for military personnel. This is not always the case for domestic law enforcement. How well the red team member has gotten into his role, given the questionable nature of the costume, is unknown. In this photograph, U.S. Air Force Staff Sergeant Phillips, an explosive ordinances and devices (EOD) specialist from the 824th Airborne Red Horse, examines a bomb attached to a simulated suicide bomber during a Safe Flag exercise at Avon Park Air Range, Florida. Safe Flag exercise is designed to ready troops to become a highly capable and responsive team when opening air bases worldwide. Courtesy of DoD/Staff Sergeant Matthew Hannen, U.S. Air Force, May 5, 2004.

scripted, or canned, plays. Working with unscripted materials or minimally scripted scenarios is called, in the field of theater, "improvisation."

Practicing through improvisation will help you solidify your character as well as give you the opportunity to interact with the rest of the red team members in a variety of circumstances. In turn, this practice will prepare you for any eventuality that might occur within the scenario of the simulation. The more time that can be spent in improvisational work, the better your preparation and the more convincing will your portrayal become within the context of the actual simulated event. Some basic improvisation rules to follow will help you to understand improvisation techniques, and following them will assist you in developing your improvisation skills more quickly.

BASIC RULES OF IMPROVISATION

1. Do not contradict the "givens" of the situation. Remain within the context of the scenario.
2. Do not contradict another character unless doing so is essential to the scenario or part of it. In other words, do not say "no," say "yes, and . . ." If someone sets up given circumstances in the improvisation situation, go along with that individual instead of contradicting him (or her) and ending the forward motion of the scenario. An example might be if another red team member, within the improvisation, asks, "Remember when we were trained together in Afghanistan?" You should not answer, "We were never trained together," because that would immediately put an end to the forward movement of the scenario. Instead, your answer might be, "Yes, I do remember that, and . . ." The second answer moves the action forward.
3. Be willing to "give up" your ideas of what you believe *should* happen, and go along with what *is happening*.
4. No matter what happens, do not "break" character. Remain in character unless the designated improvisation leader calls for a break or ends the improvisation training exercise. It is always a good policy to agree on a "safe word." This word would be called if a red team member gets hurt and needs to break character immediately or if some other situation occurs such that, for a variety of reasons, ending the improvisation might become necessary.

5. Be generous in giving others a chance to speak and
   act—as they say in the profession of acting, "Don't
   upstage the other actors," by always controlling what
   occurs.

Learning to Improvise

To learn to improvise and improve your improvisational skills,
set up exercises of varying lengths of time that have very basic
scenario outlines. Ideally, two people should lead the improvisational training exercises. One person, a tactical consultant
(someone familiar with simulation training or, even better, an
actual person from the "target group"), would be highly valuable in offering authentic interaction suggestions that would
be indicative of the terrorist group being portrayed by the red
team. A second ideal person to lead the simulation training
would be a theater professional who is skilled in teaching improvisational theater techniques. If these two individuals are
familiar with the specifics of the red team's upcoming situation and can work in concert with each other, then tactical,
cultural, and theatrical aspects of the simulations can seem authentic and approach real life.

Improvisation exercises should be of varying length, beginning with short scenes geared toward helping the red team
members become comfortable as actors and increasing in
length and difficulty as the red team members gain experience
and comfort within their characters. Final improvised scenes
might be as long as a whole afternoon or morning, or even a
full day.

It is ideal training if improvisational scenes are geared toward problem solving. For instance, if you say to a group of
red team members in training, "Let's improvise for ten minutes with you in your characters," the likelihood of success will
be minimal. A much better approach is to suggest a specific

problem to be solved. For instance, the trainer might say, "You have gathered together, in your roles, to decide who will lead your tactical maneuvers. Take ten minutes, in your characters, to discuss and make this decision." The specificity of the second suggested exercise will result in a far more successful training exercise. It will allow the red team members to focus less on acting and more on problem solving, thereby assisting them in "getting into their character," without potential self-consciousness.

After improvising each scene with other red team members, you should take the time to analyze what seemed to work and what did not seem realistic. The two leaders should offer their observations as guidance. Repetition of improvisational exercises, which increase in length and difficulty, prepares the red team members for the full-length simulation so that they can approach it with knowledge and confidence in their ability to be convincing and handle any eventuality that might be presented.

MOVING FORWARD IN BECOMING A RED TEAM MEMBER

These techniques and exercises, if fully utilized by the individual red team member and the red team as a whole, will help the "nonactor" to develop a believable character and be able to interact with others on the red team to create a realistic group of terrorists for simulation purposes. The key to the success of this venture is actually following the steps outlined. Take the time to create the file on your character, answer the important questions about your character, and think about your character in various lifelike situations. Choose photographs or pictures that help make the character become "real" for you. Remember that there are no "right" or "wrong" answers; by using your imagination within the contextual reality of the exercise, you can achieve a portrayal that, while "acting," will be extremely effective within the reality of the simulation.

The more time that the red team has to improvise, as outlined above, the better. The old adage of "practice makes perfect" is a reality with regard to the red team becoming a convincing whole rather than appearing to be just a group of individuals. Beginning with simple problem-solving improvisation exercises and building up to longer and more-complex exercises prepares red team members for the simulation exercise by building confidence and a keen knowledge base, not only of the situational elements of the exercise but also in terms of individual characters and the manner in which the group as a whole works. Shakespeare's advice to actors, as spoken through the character of Hamlet over four centuries ago, remains true today in getting the red team ready for its role, both individually and as a group: "Suit the action to the word, the word to the action." Following this guidance will result in full preparation for the task ahead.

CHAPTER 7

TERRORIST ATTACK CYCLE

They only have to get it right once; we have to get it right
every time.

—Common statement on counterterrorism

Terrorist operations can run the full gamut from the unprofessional, amateurish, and badly executed through reasonably well-planned and executed attacks to elite special forces types of activities. Fortunately, the spectrum of attacks generally shows a cluster at the unprofessional and amateurish level, occurring in ever-lower frequencies at the middle and higher levels of sophistication and professionalism. Such terrorist operations can be better understood if viewed from the context of special operations (Spec Ops) theory and practice, as articulated by William McRaven, and the OODA Loop model developed by John Boyd.[1] Professional terrorist groups and operatives more closely adhere to these theories and models and as a result are sophisticated and deadly in their operations. In some instances, terrorists will knowingly follow special forces and military planning and procedures in their attacks and understand these principles, but such theories and insights are unfamiliar to the majority of terrorists. Terrorists may, however, muddle into some of the discussed capabilities as a result of trial-and-error processes and their own doctrines, based on such works as *Military Instruction Manual* (Montoneros), *The Greenbook* (Irish Republican Army) or *The Manchester Manual*

(Al Qaeda) or tradecraft derived from closed chat rooms and group-affiliated Web sites.

Actual threat group operations can be broken down into what is called the terrorist attack cycle (TAC). Numerous attack-cycle typologies exist, with sequential and overlapping stages. Differing typologies are useful for the type and level of analysis or training being conducted. One generic typology of catastrophic terrorism (based on chemical, biological, radiological, nuclear, and [high-yield] explosives [CBRNE]) highlights the following cycle: strategy, planning, tactics, weaponization, recruitment, logistics, preparation, and execution.[2] In this work, the terrorist attack cycle is said to be composed of three main phases: planning, preparation, and execution. This typology has proven useful because of its operational simplicity and because it has been successfully used many times in simulated red team activities.[3] Each phase, in turn, will have components focusing on such considerations as weapons and equipment, reconnaissance, recruitment, and other requirements to make an operation a success.

No two groups' terrorist attack cycle will be exactly alike, as each will approach the planning, preparation, and execution phases differently. Therefore, these cycles will be influenced and modified by the thought process and value system of the threat group that will be encountered. A danger always exists in simulating terrorist activity, because a "peer competitor" approach may be taken in determining the capabilities and procedures of the opposing force. This is a common problem in U.S. defense planning. Because it can lead to "cultural threat myopia," it is something that needs to be considered when dealing with homeland security and terrorism concerns. A countering approach to the myopia issue accepts that Western, Asian, and Islamic military traditions exist and takes these into consideration when analyzing threat group approaches to suicide operations.[4] Other modifiers that may need to be considered include secular and religious group perspectives, ideologies, group organization and structure, finances, leader types and biases, and overall health of the group. As an example, pre-9/11, Al Qaeda was able to execute "spectacular" attacks—complex, deadly, and headline-worthy terrorist events. With the subsequent neutralization of Al Qaeda's bases in Afghanistan and the killing of many of the group's leaders, Al Qaeda's "health" suffered. As a result, the ability of Al Qaeda elements to coordinate such signature attacks has become greatly diminished, though they are now trying to reconstitute this capability from safe enclaves in western Pakistan, with some marginal success.

Some discussion must also be undertaken of the differences inherent in simulating the terrorist attack cycle with regard to a simple incident, an intermediate incident, complex incidents, and a full-fledged terrorist campaign. Further thoughts on how success and failure are viewed from the terrorist perspective need to be touched upon, since these greatly influence how operations are carried out and why even failed attacks can be considered successful.

SPEC OPS THEORY AND PRACTICE

The value of McRaven's Spec Ops theoretical approach is that it provides a better understanding of how a terrorist group would ideally execute a successful mission. Understanding the ideal is important because it makes all components of the terrorist attack cycle more effective. The approach focuses on the successful attributes required for a small group of operatives (such as commandos) to attack a much larger force or one deployed in an entrenched or fortified position. To be successful, the smaller force needs to acquire what is known as relative superiority, "a condition that exists when an attacking force, generally smaller, gains a decisive advantage over a larger or well-defended enemy. The value of the concept of relative superiority lies in its ability to illustrate which positive forces influence the success of the mission and to show how the frictions of war affect the achievement of the goal."[5] Three basic properties of relative superiority are viewed to exist:

1. Relative superiority is achieved at the pivotal moment in an engagement.
2. Once relative superiority is achieved, it must be sustained in order to guarantee victory.
3. If relative superiority is lost, it is difficult to regain.[6]

A sample relative superiority graph is provided in McRaven's theoretical discussion; the axes consist of probability of success and time, with the Spec Ops unit striving to cross the relative superiority line. The NLECTC–West Counter-OPFOR Program applied this concept successfully to the analysis of the 9/11 attacks, with relative superiority being gained by Al Qaeda on one of the aircraft that struck the World Trade Center towers and being first gained and then lost on the aircraft that crashed into the Pennsylvania countryside.[7]

McRaven goes on to delineate six principles that can be controlled and have an effect on relative superiority: simplicity, security, repetition, surprise, speed, and purpose. Each principle is pretty self-evident and shares a relationship to some degree or another to the nine tenets, or principles of war, utilized by the U.S. Army known by the acronym MOOSEMUSS.[8] McRaven then applies a case study approach to the theory and tests it against historical special operations missions. The value of this approach for simulation is that high-end terrorist operations will see the threat groups closely follow these principles. Very few terrorist groups, though, will carry out operations at this state-of-the-art level in their planning, preparation, and execution of a mission. Red teams must be cognizant of this fact and mimic the terrorist attack cycle at the appropriate OPFOR capabilities level.

OODA LOOPS

John Boyd's OODA (observe, orient, decide, act) Loop model explains that conflicts are time compressed; when two opponents engage each other, the combatant with the faster engagement (also viewed as reaction) cycle—all other elements being equal—will be the victor. To visualize this process, think of two competing loops that are interlocked and interact with each other. The goal is to have your loop be tighter and quicker than the loop belonging to the opposing force. The model was originally developed for Air Force fighter combat engagements but has since been applied to other areas of conflict, with the U.S. Marine Corps, in particular, being highly influenced by Boyd's work. The real-world implications are that forces that are weaker and deficient in capabilities can, by speeding up their engagement cycle, defeat superior opponents. The intent is for a force to shorten its loops and pull ahead of its opponent, thus using action to beat reaction and operationally disrupting and paralyzing opponents. A historical example of this approach to conflict can be seen with the German blitzkrieg launched against France in 1940.

For terrorism purposes, if an OPFOR can launch a campaign against a city, region, or state and sufficiently get ahead in its engagement cycle, then the responding forces will fall further and further behind in their response capabilities. This is one of the dangers that now exist for the Mexican government with regard to the drug wars within that country, and it has direct homeland security implications for the United States. The cartels are intentionally bribing and assassinating police officers, judges, and politicians in some regions of Mexico far more quickly now, to become fully entrenched in local society before they can be rooted out. The OODA Loop model has also been applied to school active-shooter countermeasures. Direct Measures International, Inc., utilizes the OODA Loop in its steps to crisis response with the goal of separating students from the threat as the main objective by utilizing fortification and evacuation techniques.[9] Thus, both the allied force and the OPFOR utilize and benefit from this model. This model obviously overlaps with the relative superiority concepts discussed earlier and should be used to complement them when thinking about the terrorist attack cycle.

PHASES OF THE TERRORIST ATTACK CYCLE

The Planning Phase

The planning phase, much like the observe (who/what) and orient (where/when) steps of the OODA Loop, represents the first phase of the terrorist attack cycle. It is followed by the preparation (OODA: decide [how/why] step) and execution (OODA: act [as trained] step) phases. This first phase determines what the operation is going to be and how it should be carried out. Terrorist planning is determined partly by individual group structures; as a result, advanced terrorist network modeling has been undertaken for the Futures Working Group (FWG). This modeling suggests that with differing forms of group structures come four identifiable types of OPFOR leadership. These forms of leadership and the structures they are found within engage in diverse command and control processes. Such processes in turn influence group planning, preparation, and execution of terrorist acts.

Direct control leaders. The first type of leadership exists from a "tightly coupled" perspective—that is, leadership derived from detailed instruction and control. These are direct managers of violence who give specific orders to others and watch over them to ensure that those directives are precisely carried out. These direct control leaders are primarily found in hub nodes that follow hierarchical and industrial processes based on tasks.

Network influence leaders. The second type of leaders transmit their commander's intent to their followers, who then seek to fulfill the mission. These network influence leaders may be found in hub nodes but may also be found in mesh and to a lesser extent still-immature all-channel networks. Tolerance exists for the tasks undertaken to achieve this goal, with some self-organizing behavior being evident. Those directed take on the role of independent contractors more than that of employees.

Collective vision leaders. The third leader type is based on an even more extreme and evolved form of decentralized control, and leaders of this type exist in mesh and all-channel networks that have developed a network or collective vision. Commander's intent is no longer required, from a leadership perspective. This network vision of the mission or end state is recognized and shared by all the nodal members, each of whom influences it and is in turn influenced by it. These collective vision leaders may shift leadership roles to engage in specialized activities and if evolved enough have the capability to engage in swarming behavior. To these entities, symbols of rank and authority are no longer required and are generally ignored.

Isolated leaders. The fourth leader type is based on the existence of an individual who functions as a true force-of-one. These leaders exist only in no-channel networks that are so decentralized as to operate on the edge of chaos and anarchy. Examples would be the Phineas Priests and Al Qaeda affinity members engaging in lone wolf behavior derived from the principles of "leaderless resistance." The higher end state sought or mission of the network in these examples is, however, derived in two very completely different ways. In the case of the Phineas Priests, a simple prime directive or raison d'être exists—engage in any violent activity against nonwhites. In the case of Al Qaeda no-channel affinity node members, the end state is transmitted by network influence leaders such as Osama Bin Laden or Ayman al-Zawahiri.[10]

For actual terrorist planning, the key personnel are direct control leaders for group operations and isolated leaders for lone wolf operations. Network vision leaders may inspire the planners to attack infidels or give their blessing to conduct specific operations, but they should be viewed as strategic rather than operational-level leaders. Collective vision leaders would be found with "flash mobs" and likeminded gang or group members such as anarchists or skinheads, but the mesh and all-channel networks of these entities have not shown themselves to be evolved enough currently to carry out terrorist operations. For proactive law enforcement missions, terrorist group operations, especially for mid- and low-level groups, have a far better chance of being interdicted than do lone wolf operations, because far more personnel are required and more communications take place and the former's operation will generally require a larger logistical footprint.

During this phase, the mission, in terms of what or who will be attacked and by what means, will be decided upon. For terrorist groups, the rational choice is that mission intent and target set should drive the planning, but many times a group will get good at one form of attack or a type of attack becomes their signature or calling card. For example, Hamas, at its terrorist peak, focused on killing people on public buses by means of sending suicide bombers onto them, while Hezbollah utilized explosive-laden car and truck bombs to damage and take down buildings. Some violent antiabortion groups may only vandalize or bomb clinics but for whatever reason do not assassinate the doctors performing abortions, while others do carry out assassinations. Even Al Qaeda has fallen into the need to launch "spectaculars," when a couple of small-scale mall bombings would probably serve just as well to generate immense amounts of terror in the United States or Western Europe.

During this phase, surveillance on potential targets is conducted. This will almost always be done physically by visiting the target, but such surveillance can now be augmented by such virtual tools as Google Earth or actual venue, hobbyist, and even vacation Web sites, which may contain quite a bit of intelligence on the possible target. If a public-venue reconnaissance can be done fairly safely and if concern exists for OPSEC, those doing the initial scouting can only be used for that aspect of the operation. The planning for large operations may take weeks if not a few months of target selection, whereas for a small operation it may take only days. For a lone wolf (or hasty) attack, twenty minutes or less looking over the potential target may be all that is required. Factors influencing target selection will include openness and hardness of the target, avenues of approach, ability to egress after the operation (for nonsuicide forces), symbolic or functional value, and media and body count potentials.

Once the target is determined, then an attack plan needs to be created. This can range from a highly detailed document, much like a computerized mission folder, to a midrange document written in a notebook with some sketches and pictures to a verbal five-paragraph order based on a few notes, or it can even consist of just a mental image belonging to a deranged person with a gun. Too much complexity can kill an operation, while, at the other extreme, too little planning might have the would-be terrorist show up at a closed venue or one swarming with patrol officers and emergency personnel conducting a drill. To be most successful, terrorist planning should just be good enough to get the mission done with a slight margin for error. The plan itself is basically how to kill, injure, or kidnap people; damage or destroy buildings, infrastructure, or materiel; or target anything else of value, such as crops or animals. A very simple plan would be to take father's gun, do an ammo check, put in backpack, walk to school, wait until third period, take out gun, and shoot fellow classmates. Far more elaborate plans may call for substantial resources to be expended and training to be conducted to successfully carry off the mission. In fact, for more-specialized weaponry such as man-portable air defense systems (MANPADS) and even rocket-propelled grenades (RPGs), the planning document had better account for personnel training for these systems in addition to obtaining these systems in the first place and getting them to the country where the attack will be taking place. More than one terrorist incident has failed because a MANPADS was fired at a plane at a low altitude, giving the missile warhead no time to arm, or because an RPG was fired at a vehicle but still had the protective fuse cap on, making the device inert.

The Preparation Phase

Once the operational plan has been created, preparations are needed to generate the capability to carry it out. One of the best overviews of the more formal process used by sophisticated terrorist groups can be found in various chapters of Malcolm Nance's updated *Terrorist Recognition Handbook.*[11] The actual scope of the logistics and training required in preparation for a specific terrorist operation or school shooting, however, greatly varies. Established terrorist groups engaging in an insurgency type of campaign, such as the Irish Republican Army (IRA) during its active period, have a well-developed infrastructure in place. Safe houses, secret armories, bomb factories, motor pools, and training facilities (sometimes underground) are already in existence. In addition, financial resources gained by means of charitable front organizations and ongoing criminal activities (such as robberies, drug sales, extortion, and street taxation) provide the ability to purchase materials, pay facility rents and costs, and financially support full-time group members.

This same level of infrastructure development is also apparent for other terrorist organizations such as Hezbollah, elements of Al Qaeda, and Mexican drug cartel enforcers such as Los Zetas, Los Negros, Los Numeros, Kaibiles, and various *sicarios* (assassins) although, in the case of the cartels, front charities are not utilized to generate income. All of these organizations with well-developed infrastructures have active and reserve (or sleeper) cells with general and specialized capabilities. An active cell near the selected target can be utilized or brought in from another area, a reserve cell can be activated, or an entirely new cell can be created for the mission. These groups will conduct training and actual rehearsals for the mission, continue with surveillance and reconnaissance of the target as required, and be able to obtain weapons and transport by requisitioning them from stores. For specialized weapons, technologies, disguises, and documents, group units can create, procure, or steal them from third parties. If such preparations appear to mimic the capabilities of an underground military organization, it is because that is exactly what they represent. Professional terrorists and former special forces personnel who have gone over to the drug cartels essentially function as nonstate or criminal soldiers and may possess military capabilities that rival or surpass those of some nation-states.

Where the preparation phase gets somewhat more drawn out is with mid- and lower-level terrorist organizations and isolated cells (or hierarchical hub nodes) that either do not have the direct support of a large terrorist organization or are operating independently from it. This would characterize an affinity group, a gang of guys, fragments of a group, or a newer group working its way up. Once these groups have the developed ops plan in hand, they will likely have to build up their capability to carry out the mission. This can be a daunting process for such entities, and numerous mistakes can be made, which provides opportunities for law enforcement to interdict the operation during this phase. Even a group such as the Aum Shinrikyo (Supreme Truth) cult in Japan, with its deep financial resources and intellectual resources (lots of science PhDs but with no real-world small unit experience), made numerous mistakes during this phase with its WMD and advanced technology (high-power laser) weaponization attempts. For these groups, petty crimes may be conducted to generate cash and income for actual weapons or weapon component procurement, training, surveillance, and day-to-day group living expenses. New recruits may need to be brought into the group and socialized into its value system and worldview and then, like the rest of the members, trained to conduct the operation. This training may take place overseas in terrorist training camps, locally in some sort of remote location, or at legitimate training facilities such as shooting ranges or gun clubs for tactical firearms training. In the latter case, ethnically diverse threat group members and even heavily tattooed white supremacists may be unwilling to train at such facilities because of OPSEC concerns. Members with former military, police, or security training will be highly valued and will share their knowledge and skills with the rest of the group. Whether one or more actual mission rehearsals can be conducted is at times questionable but will generally be strived for by these groups. In worst-case scenarios, sand drawings, tabletop mockups, or posters with individual member locations, movements, and responsibilities may have to suffice.

Anytime these mid- and low-level groups can get financial, equipment, training, or intelligence support from benefactor terrorist and political groups via "the enemy of my enemy is my friend" dictum, they will greatly benefit. In fact, because of the marginal capabilities of these groups, such support can go a long way toward future mission success and is one of the reasons why we see so many reports of different terrorist groups networking and sharing information and other resources among themselves. This is one of the reasons why IRA members and former Israeli security personnel have appeared in South American jungles and Al Qaeda central members have linked up with affiliated terrorist groups globally.

In some ways, the preparation phase once again becomes relatively easier when lone wolf terrorists and active shooters are
considered. They conduct operations on the cheap; because of
that, a very small to almost untraceable logistical footprint may
exist during the preparation phase. Emotional cues, written or
verbal threats, bizarre online postings or warnings, or drawings of killings may be the only signature of an impending
attack, although purchases of police scanners, propane tanks,
road flares, black powder, body armor, guns, and ammunition
may have to occur in preparation for the mission.

Some disagreement exists among and between counterterrorism scholars and practitioners as to when the preparation
phase ends and the execution phase begins. One viewpoint
is that when the actual assault, final movement to deploy the
truck or car bomb, or final positioning of the WMD device
takes place, the execution phase has been entered. Another
viewpoint is that when all preparations have been completed,
the terrorist group has then transitioned into the execution
phase. For the purposes of simulating the terrorist attack cycle,
we will go with the second perspective on this.

The Execution Phase

When all preparations have been made, various activities may
or may not take place, depending on the type and sophistication of the attack, the nuances of the target, and the preferences of the group carrying out the incident. If specialized
external support to the group carrying out the planned attack
was utilized—such as a bomb maker on contract or from another cell of the terrorist group—those personnel will leave the
operational area or possibly even remove themselves from the
country in which the attack is going to take place. Sometimes
an operational coordinator or planner may also come in to fa-
cilitate the initial activities, and these individuals will need to

leave the area also. Both patterns have been evident for some of the Al Qaeda bombings that have transpired in the past.

For larger operations, the terrorist group may also go "dark" for the last twenty-four to forty-eight hours prior to the launch of the attack. Surveillance, reconnaissance, and outside communication would all be discontinued. This is done in the hope that countersurveillance or counterintelligence units are not alerted that the targeted facility may be imminently threatened. In that case, group members would rest and relax or potentially even engage in some wild partying. For attacks carried out by foreign jihadi groups in which suicide bombings are commonly used, the future martyrs may have a celebratory photo taken or a testimonial videotaped, may engage in ritual cleansing and prayer, and may even give away the last of their possessions. Groups that are even more sophisticated may engage in physical and media (for example, Internet videos) deception operations at the strategic or operational levels to throw off defending groups as to the actual nature and geographic venue of a coming attack. At the other extreme, while less common, physical or Internet surveillance may be continually carried out by a threat group prior to the actual attack. An example would be an observation post set up and continually manned in a rented apartment down the street from the targeted facility or venue.

Before the assault and supporting forces move on to their targets, last-minute equipment and weapons checks will be made. Typically, a safe house or safe houses will be used to stage from for the more sophisticated attacks and a motor pool will be required to get to the venue in question. At the other end of the spectrum, a teen active shooter may store his gear in the closet of his bedroom or at a drop location near the school being targeted and will take his own vehicle or the family car or even just walk to the targeted facility. Foreign operations that are more sophisticated have scouting personnel moving ahead of the assault force; their function is to alert the main element to military and law enforcement threats as it moves toward the target. In the case of a suicide bombing, the actual bomber and handler may be flanked or followed by armed security, with another scout trailing much farther behind to ensure that the assault team is not being followed and that a clear escape and evasion path exists after the actual bombing takes place. This is a manpower- and logistics-intensive type of operation and probably something very unlikely to take place in the United States, short of a major venue or gathering being attacked by a foreign terrorist group.

The more sophisticated the operation, the greater the likelihood that the videotaping of the incident will at least be discussed, if not actually done, by the group involved in carrying out the attack. Static taping via an observation post or by personnel with handheld or tripod-mounted recorders in an overwatch position is extremely easy to undertake. The other option for a terrorist group is to conduct an attack in such a way or against such public targets as to get those being attacked to tape the event so that private news media groups acquire the footage for mass broadcasting. An example might be to detonate a weak device to get all eyes and recorders on the initial incident and follow it up with a much larger secondary device in the same vicinity. Some analysts have speculated that the timing of the 9/11 attacks on the Twin Towers was intentionally done in a "one-two punch" combination for maximum media coverage, though this level of coordination seems too daunting to achieve. Regardless, the images of the second plane striking the South Tower represent the equivalent of a terrorist Pulitzer Prize in photography.

Once the initial bombing or assault is carried out during the execution phase, the terrorist cycle will then take different paths depending on the intent and structure of the operation. If a lone suicide bomber or active shooter is involved, then a martyrdom or suicide operation is in effect. No further plans have been made to egress from the attack or engage in escape and evade tactics: unless the bomb malfunctions or the shooter has a change of heart, the operation is over. In contrast, if scouts, armed security, a handler, and propaganda (videotaping the incident) personnel are supporting a suicide bomber, then they would all be required to escape and evade from the bombing site, and the operation would not be over until they had safely fled the scene, had been captured, or were killed. Secondary and tertiary bombs or attacks may be part of the mission, with or without a martyrdom or suicide component. In the case of a modified hostage-taking incident, the terrorists may barricade and fortify in place with the hostages and draw in the media so that their demands can be made known, or they may simply start to kill people on camera for shock effect once enough video recorders are pointing their way. From a more conventional terrorist group perspective, assault and bombings may be designed so that all those involved with the event have at least the chance to come out of it alive. In such a case, escape and evasion plans with fallback rendezvous points and safe houses or means to get out of the country will have been thought out in detail.

Of all the ways to execute a terrorist operation, by far one of the most difficult to stop and respond to is what is known as a "contextual attack." Bunker utilized this technique in the food court of a major mall while engaging in counterterrorism training. Basically, the argument for this approach is that attacks and attackers that mimic their surroundings have the lowest probability of being viewed as an anomaly or threat. Being within the context of your environment—in terms of your dress, ethnic profile, mannerisms and behaviors, cover story (if needed), and actions—makes a terrorist pretty much invisible. Any actions that you take or items that you utilize in that environment will be given the benefit of the doubt by others in that environment, by both the public and security personnel. When others look at you, they will attempt to place you, your actions, and items in context.

A public shopping mall provides a good example. A terrorist who intends to bomb a mall with a backpack bomb has many

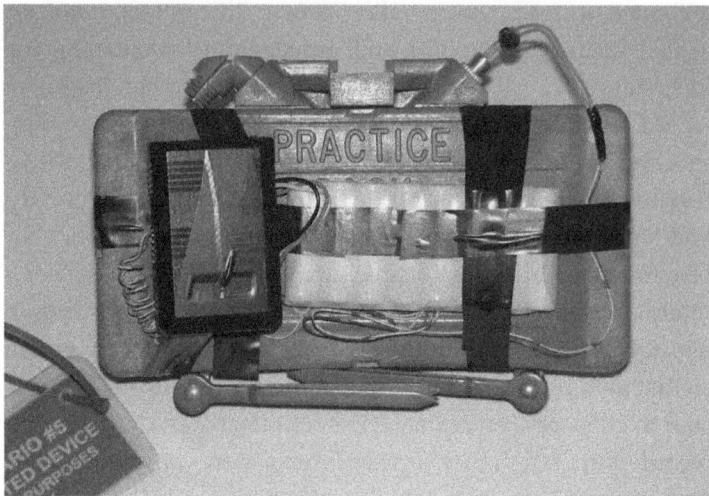

A training device (an improvised claymore antipersonnel mine) used in a terrorism exercise in Florida. The device was placed inside of a Wendy's bag in the bleachers of a football stadium. The bag was out of context, because the stadium did not contain a Wendy's concession, and also was positioned oddly. Therefore, the responding forces should have immediately considered the bag and its contents highly suspect. Courtesy of David Kuhn.

options. One option is to leave the backpack on or under a bench in the covered walkways of the mall where people walk back and forth in front of the many interior mall stores. However, a backpack left in this context all alone will immediately come to the attention of mall shoppers, security, and even petty thieves. The dwell time for such a backpack with an IED in it is almost nonexistent and would not give a bomber much time to leave the mall before it would be flagged as a threat, removed, or stolen. If, in contrast, a backpack with an IED in it is left in a food court under a table with a chair pulled out, a partially eaten meal on the table (minus the drink), and a coat draped over the back of the chair, the context in which the backpack is now in totally changes.[12] An observer would naturally think that someone must be eating lunch and has gone to get a drink refill. In such instances, a much longer dwell time exists for such a backpack IED, because the backpack makes sense given the surroundings and context in which it exists.

Other counterterrorism professionals have used similar techniques in training. Of course, a "contextual attack" using a suicide bomber disguised as a pregnant women near a mall or a rabbi near a synagogue has almost no dwell time near the target. The window of vulnerability of such an attack to be foiled is even shorter because all the bomber has to do is walk to the target spot and self-detonate. Still, once an attack force is out of context—it is no longer stealth masked—the clock is running on an operation because those around that force or object will label it as a potential or confirmed threat and alert the authorities. Heavily armed men running into a high school are thus at the opposite extreme in executing an operation. In such a "stand-up assault," speed, shock, and blatant force rather than hiding in plain sight are used to gain the initiative. More sophisticated terrorist groups will, of course, know how to utilize both approaches—and other ones based on "infiltration" (commando) or "stand-off" (long-range weapons) techniques—and how to leverage all of these approaches to produce operational synergies.

SIMPLE INCIDENTS, INTERMEDIATE INCIDENTS, AND TERRORIST CAMPAIGNS

The terrorist attack cycle discussed above is basically a linear and noniterated process. A terrorist group will go from phase A to B to C with the components of each phase also generally following a linear pattern, though some tasks within a phase (such as obtaining weapons, recruitment, and indoctrination) can be overlapping or even take place simultaneously with each other. Simple incidents are relatively basic in that the law enforcement or military response follows its own preincident, transincident, and postincident phases in a similar phase A to B to C process. The terrorist attack cycle and the responding force process when viewed from the perspective of the OODA Loop model can thus be seen as two competing loops that are interlocked and interact with each other.

In simulating this interaction for responses to terrorism, the focus can be placed on simple incidents at either the pre- or transincident phases for law enforcement and other responders. An example of this type of incident would be that of a lone suicide bomber planning to detonate himself on a bus or two active shooters committing multiple homicides in a high school. If focused on the transincident responder phase, this will correlate with the execution phase for a terrorist group. If focused on the preincident responder phase, this will correlate with either the planning or the preparation phase for a terrorist group. For simple incidents, the postincident response phase is not normally simulated, because for response forces this essentially becomes a consequence management mission.

Intermediate incidents result in what could be called semi-iterated operations. These are slightly more difficult to simulate because the terrorist execution phase is spread out temporally—purposeful lag times between attacks exist—instead of the attacks all taking place at once. If these lag times are relatively short, then law enforcement will still respond as if a simple incident were taking place. As an example, one suicide bomber plans to detonate and, in the process, the rest of the surviving crowd is driven toward another suicide bomber, who will detonate a few minutes later at a choke point full of escaping victims. Where this gets slightly trickier to simulate is when a simple terrorist incident of some sort has taken place and the law enforcement and other responders have entered the postincident phase, then are themselves attacked. A good example would be a scenario in which a suicide bombing took place and the response forces have arrived and are tending to the casualties with a perimeter set, active triage and medical transport taking place, and a command post established. A sniper is then added to the simulation and begins to fire on the responding forces. The responding forces now not only are conducting postincident operations (albeit in a highly disrupted manner) but have also entered back into the transincident phase and are forced to immediately engage in active operations against the sniper. The lesson here is that the more phases taking place simultaneously for the responding forces, the more complexity is brought into the simulation.

Simulations become extremely complex when multiple terrorist assaults are planned. These operations can take place simultaneously across a geographic area (multiple incidents timed to take place all at once) or in a campaign mode with the incidents spread out over geography and time. Such complex attacks and terrorist campaigns result in fully iterated operations taking place. Each tactical engagement becomes a set battle in larger operations and begins to closely mimic a military engagement between opposing forces. Multiple terrorist attack cycles come into play, as do multiple law enforcement and military response cycles. The Mumbai attacks in India in November 2008 provide a recent example of such complex operations. The attacks were carried out by radical Islamist terrorists linked to groups in Pakistan. They consisted of a combination of bombings, stand-up assaults, and hostage barricade incidents that lasted for four days. A period of relative superiority was initially gained by the terrorist forces at the beginning of their assaults. Although this advantage was eventually lost because of the sheer mass of the responding forces, it helped to give the equivalent of a squad-size group of men the ability to disrupt and paralyze a city of over thirteen million people for a few days.

If such a campaign were to be launched on U.S. soil, not only would ongoing transincident response and consequence management operations be taking place during and after each incident, but also ongoing proactive measures, such as suspected safe house raids and monitoring, analysis, and coordination of metropolitan resources for intelligence and threat analysis (plus futures) would be undertaken around the clock. Even generically simulating multiple terrorist assaults and terrorist campaigns can, however, easily get into a gray area of sensitivity concerning domestic response capabilities. For this reason, higher-level operations and complex simulations are considered outside of the scope and intent of this work (but see appendix 1 and appendix 2 for examples of two simulation types).

SUCCESS AND FAILURE ARE DETERMINED BY THE OBSERVER

One of the most difficult situations for responders is to acknowledge that even a failed attack taking place during the execution phase can in many instances still be considered a success for a terrorist group. This can be extremely upsetting for the responding forces if dwelled upon, because it can create no-win situations for them and the communities and nation that they serve. This perspective emotionally hit home for Bunker during a red team debrief in which a cell advisor—who had much European experience with counterterrorism operations—was consoling, in role-playing mode, the cell team leader who was in charge of a failed assault. The cell leader was very emotional that team members had been lost in what, from a military perspective, was a badly executed amateur attack that was beaten back and did not complete its mission. The cell advisor calmly turned this logic on its head and explained that a great victory had been achieved over the infidels. Two members of the cell had been martyred in the assault, and the targeted forces had been made to know fear because of the power and righteousness of the group's activities.

As Westerners accustomed to a perspective more in line with General George S. Patton's famous, though misattributed, quotation, "I want you to remember that no bastard ever won a war by dying for his country. He won it by making the other poor, dumb bastard die for his country,"[13] accepting such logic can be extremely difficult. But when analyzed properly, terrorist assaults, even failed ones, can be seen to highlight group dedication to the cause and can readily result in increased group notoriety and media exposure. This translates into more opportunities for successful recruitment, financial and material support, and community goodwill among their constituents. Failed attacks also provide other benefits such as community and societal disruption—the general spreading of terror among those targeted—and may prompt an overreaction by a government, which may in turn alienate citizens and push them into the radicalized camps. For simulation purposes, this means that terrorist attacks may be launched without ever hoping to succeed. As long as they can be hastily executed, the level of sophistication is inconsequential and any mission goals beyond causing simple mayhem for a sustained period are irrelevant. This is one way to look at the doomed Tet Offensive of 1968 carried out by the Vietcong and North Vietnamese Army. In this light, numerous unsuccessful attacks, and possibly even a few successes, can in an insurgency situation, as was waged in Vietnam, potentially lead to victory: "'You know you never defeated us on the battlefield,' said the American colonel. The North Vietnamese colonel pondered this remark a moment. 'That may be so,' he replied, 'but it is also irrelevant.'"[14]

The lesson learned from this analysis is that terrorists need to be interdicted and stopped in the planning and preparation phases of the attack cycle and not allowed to enter the execution phase, because at that point, the response has come too late: even if the assault fails, the terrorists may have succeeded simply through the act of launching the assault. This puts the onus on domestic U.S. responding forces to take the initiative and better develop their intelligence capabilities and on those engaged in supporting training and exercises to create terrorist simulations that stress proactive measures over execution-phase responses.

CHAPTER 8

Future Terrorism

Out-Innovating the Terrorists

We don't have to get the future right, just less wrong than
our opponents.

—BlackFor military analyst, 1998

There are many pitfalls in seeking to assess future trends in terrorists' tactics, strategies, motivations, and capabilities. Given
their often-clandestine nature and the fact that they may
change in regard to both short-term developments and long-
term trends that evolve slowly, plotting the future terrorist
landscape and those involved in it is not easy. Further, terrorists are innovative and often unconstrained by the cumbersome
processes that are part and parcel of the complexity of modern states and corporations and often act as an impediment to
change. As noted earlier, small may be beautiful but unfortunately also lethal in asymmetric conflicts, in which the size and
complexity and power of an adversary are changed into liabilities. One must recognize that one is gazing into a very clouded
looking glass. Despite this, however, there is also continuity.
Terrorists may be innovative but will also rely on traditional
means of engaging in carnage. The assault rifle and bomb will
remain major weapons in their arsenal even as other weaponry
achieves greater precision and destructive power.

Despite the challenges inherent in peering into the future,
such an analysis can provide early-warning insights for both
large and small organizations. Although no one can see the
future with complete accuracy, that is not the intent of such an

effort. Rather, the intent is for our law enforcement and military forces to make fewer mistakes about the future than the opposing forces. This will allow our forces to better prepare—via simulations and training derived from projected threat scenarios and emergent environments—for future operations.

Out-innovating the terrorists can be achieved by drawing upon the disciplines of both early-warning analysis and futures research. Early-warning analysis is normally used to scan the event horizon to look for signs of an impending threat or attack. Tactical and operationally focused groups generally are concerned with near-term attack potentials, whereas strategically focused groups will scan for long-term threats.[1] The changing capability and intent of opposing entities along with their evolution and morphing from one type of group to another are forms of continual concern. Scanning for near and distant threats represents a defensive perspective and looks to mitigate future potentials for damage and harm. For counterterrorism purposes, this form of analysis looks out to the future and then links back to the now. It results in the creation of new defenses, countermeasures, and courses of action so that the responding forces can disrupt, preempt, mitigate, and neutralize future attacks and threats. Futures research, in contrast, is primarily a projection of past trends and typically looks out beyond five years "to deal with social problems in original and novel ways. The three primary goals of futures research are to form perceptions of the future (the possible), study likely alternatives (the probable), and make choices to bring about particular events (the preferable)."[2] For counterterrorism purposes, the futures approach thus starts with the now and branches off into alternative futures, with the intent of shaping the actual future in such a way as to most benefit the responding forces' capabilities. Equally important, it represents an offensive perspective (though not normally expressed in such terms), because it looks to better an organization's position through the future shaping and manipulation of its environment, opponents, and itself.

We thus see immense value in both early-warning analysis and futures research for counterterrorism purposes. We argue that, in order to effectively out-innovate the terrorists, both the offensive and the defensive dynamics of these disciplines need to be harnessed so that threats can be detected and desirable futures shaped in a coordinated manner. To that end, seven major future simulation needs have been identified. These needs, as expected, will at times overlap because of collinear trends and overlapping categories. In identifying these needs, the authors are generating the most probable requirements for terrorist simulations in the coming years and beyond. While we do not expect to get the future "right," our intent is to simply get it less wrong than our opponents, and in the process, aid US law enforcement and military responding forces in out-innovating the terrorists.

FUTURE SIMULATIONS

Directed Energy and Other Forms of Advanced and Exotic Weaponry

The evolutionary use patterns of military and criminal arms suggest that terrorists will increasingly utilize more-advanced and exotic forms of weaponry. While terrorists predominately rely on the gun and the bomb in their assaults and attacks, these patterns of use will slowly be modified by the transition in military weaponry from firearms and explosives to directed energy weapons. Directed energy weapons offer a host of new and desirable military capabilities including extreme standoff ranges, no time-of-flight or ballistic limitations, and a "deep clip" (since an energy source rather than rounds are utilized). Bunker has studied opposing-force incidents and potentials of counteroptical (vision disrupting and blinding) lasers for over a decade; it is no longer a question of *if* terrorists will use laser weapons, as some have already made attempts in this regard.[3] As early as the mid-1990s, for example, the Japanese Aum Shin-rikyo cult failed in its attempt to use a laser weapon against police forces. Numerous incidents of laser use by insurgents, Mexican drug cartel enforcers, and foreign militaries have been documented, along with the use of lasers by Greek anarchists in December 2008 during urban rioting, and these set the stage for more incidents to come.

During this transition in military weaponry, we are now see-ing the emergence of combined or hybrid systems that utilize both firearms and laserarms (directed energy) components. At the most basic level, this will mean that laser sights fitted to firearms will become more prevalent for kinetic targeting pur-poses. Midrange systems will provide tandem "soft-kill and hard-kill" capabilities—a target once visually disrupted by a laser, and basically defenseless, is much easier to kill. A few high-end systems may even have the ability to blind and/or kill by means of the laser alone and also kill by means of the firearm attachment. Traditional firearms and bombs may be utilized in conjunction with these hybrid systems; on the other end of the continuum, stand-alone directed energy systems, such as the Chinese ZM-87 laser blinder, may also be used in a combined arms manner. Laser weapons also have the ability to disrupt and blind cameras and other forms of electro-optical sensors and even start fires at long distances. For simulation purposes, this means that at some point directed energy weap-ons will need to be considered for scenario inclusion. One area of ongoing concern is the targeting of commercial and airborne law enforcement aircraft by lasers—loss of vision for pilots is the specific safety issue. In addition to lasers, other forms of di-rected energy weapons based on radio frequency, high-power microwave, and millimeter wave devices also exist. They too will need to be considered for simulation purposes, but as a follow-on to the more immediate concern of laser threats simulation.

In addition to concerns about directed energy weapons, two other weaponry trends need to be considered. First, more exotic forms of infantry small arms and improvised explosive devices exist than have so far been utilized in terrorist incidents perpetrated inside the United States. Whereas some of these conventional weaponry contingencies (such as suicide bombers, vehicle-borne improvised explosive devices [VBIEDs], 50-caliber sniper rifles, man-portable air defense systems [MANPADS], and rocket-propelled grenades [RPGs])—are already recognized and are being incorporated into training, others (such as collar bombs, internal body bombs, platter charges, and thermobaric explosives) have not.[4] Some determination needs to be made as to when and if such other forms of exotic weaponry will be included in training and simulations.

Second, and probably more important, tele-operated (or remotely operated) weapons have emerged. They are now being used by the U.S. military in static mount and on ground robot and remotely piloted vehicles. These systems are controlled by either hard-line or wireless communication network computer interfaces. The weapon and its movements, in turn, are manipulated by basic joystick, gamelike console, or virtual reality (glove and headset or Wii-like) controllers linked to the computer system. Commercial emergence of a similar system in 2005 is quite significant: "Internet hunting, also called 'cyber hunting' or 'computer assisted remote hunting,' allows a person with an Internet connection to fire a rifle from anywhere, killing real prey in real time."[5] Although dozens of state bans against such hunting have been enacted and the initial Live-Shot.com Web site with its Remington .30-06 rifle–controlled weapon is no longer active, the terrorist potentials offered by this technology are blatantly apparent.[6] By substituting humans for animals as the target, one can cheaply create virtual reach-back capability for operational support. For this reason, simulation of this technology in terrorism scenarios needs to be considered a near-term imperative.

These types of insurgent weapons could someday be used inside the United States; it is far better to train against and simulate these weapons in exercises now rather than after they have been utilized. The photograph shows RPGs and a launcher and other weapons acquired by U.S. Marines from insurgents who attacked the police station in Al Kharma, Iraq, during security and stabilization operations (SASO) in Al Anbar Province in support of Operation Iraqi Freedom. *Top to bottom:* USSR RKG-3 hand grenade *(left)*, AK-47 clips *(right)*; RPG-7 launcher; PG-7VM HEAT grenade; Chinese 75 mm, HE-T, Type 69 grenade; two USSR PG-7G HEAT-T grenades; PG-7VM HEAT grenade; AK-47 without stock. Courtesy of DoD/Lance Corporal Jordan F. Sherwood, USMC, June 8, 2004.

Along with the realization that new and exotic weapons need to be included in future terrorism simulations comes the recognition of the importance of technicians. A vital need now exists to integrate and test the ability of technicians as an intimate part of the response team rather than solely using them in an advisory role. Some of the workings and nuances of these weapons and technologies are only understood by governmental and industry lab scientists and academics in specialized settings. While many might argue that such a policy further blurs the line between responders (combatants) and civilians (noncombatants), in the case of terrorism such artificialities of international law were long ago abandoned by the perpetrators. As a nation, the United States should harness all of its scientific and technical assets and consider them an integral part of its multidisciplinary responding forces.

Threat Group Dual-Dimensional and Cyberspace Operations

For some time now, cyberspace has been recognized as the new "high ground" in terrorism. Advanced operations are now able to take place that leverage synergies inherent in humanspace (the traditional battlefield) and cyberspace (the emergent battlefield) in a combined dual-dimensional manner. Virtual reach-back (maintaining a real-time link to units who provide operational direct support) for intelligence, the use of computer viruses or denial-of-service attacks in support of an operation, and setting up a remotely operated weapon for "cover fire" are but a few examples of the synergies that can be produced. Both force-multiplier effects and new capabilities will be realized from such dual-dimensional operations. A few additional examples would be the following:

> The use of the Internet during an incident to create rumors, especially in terms of the magnitude of the threat and the inability of the authorities to counter the threat, which thereby cause the perception of state repression and overreaction. Terrorists will specifically use "guilt transfer" as a means of attempting to blame the authorities and the victims for the incident.
> The use of the Internet, small television cameras, low-power TV, and other forms of visual technology to create or "edit" existing visual coverage in an attempt to "stage manage" an incident from a distance.

The increasing use of individuals trained in mass media—print and electronic—as part of the assault force. In effect, these individuals will be the equivalent of the authorities' public affairs officers.

In addition, from a pure cyberspace (emergent battlefield) perspective, the following issues and threats related to future terrorist operations also need to be considered:

The increasing use of the Internet as a means of generating fear through disinformation campaigns;

The use of Internet-based deception campaigns to mask terrorist intentions and to confuse authorities;

The increasing use of the Internet as an alternative form of mass media to "inform" and "confuse" both the public and authorities;

The use of emergent virtual worlds, such as Second Life, for propaganda, recruitment, and fund-raising purposes as those virtual worlds gain in social, political, and economic importance with increasing numbers of participants; and

The launching of attacks in virtual worlds, such as embassy protests and limited instances of economic terrorism—where virtual-based retail stores have been attacked by means of an aircraft crashing into them and arson—that have already taken place.

As can be seen, a well-defined need exists to incorporate into simulations threat group–based dual-dimensional operations and cyberspace operations. One specific concern focuses on the ability during the preincident phase to counter Internet warfare waged by terrorists. This would entail testing the ability of authorities to effectively engage in cutting through Internet deception campaigns to ascertain indicators and warnings (I&W) of an imminent attack. Another concern is for authorities to develop the ability to identify, record, and counter alternative visual and mass media on a tactical and strategic level. This would allow for the creation of a "counter-stage" capability to limit terrorist propaganda and disruptive targeting effects.

Community-Based Sensor Networks and Advanced Technology

Increasingly, information and sensor technologies are being utilized by police departments of major metropolitan areas to limit crimes in commercial area such as outside bars and in downtown shopping districts. These technologies are also being utilized for criminal investigative purposes after a crime has been committed. Typically, these systems consist of stationary and pan-and-zoom-capable cameras whose images are fed into centralized viewing stations at law enforcement facilities. Backup recordings of the images stored for two weeks or more are retained before being purged, in case a crime was found to be committed within the viewing areas of the camera systems. Newer systems are Web-enabled and can be viewed and controlled (for example, the pan-and-zoom cameras can be manipulated) from laptops and distributed workstations.

Much media attention has been focused on these systems with regard to the Madrid train bombings of 2004 and the London subway bombings of 2005. Law enforcement accessed the images for postblast forensic and investigative purposes to determine the identities of the bombers, their methods, routes taken, and whether an earlier dry run had been undertaken. While these systems have been a boon to criminal intelligence collection after the fact, their true potentials are not being fully exploited. Rather than looking backwards in time, these systems should be considered for real-time use and tested in counterterrorism simulations as a proof-of-concept. Already, some cities are linking acoustic gunfire detectors to their community-based sensor networks, and others are placing motion and infrared "alerts" on their cameras, which will then automatically key the camera to the disturbance and notify the human monitors of the anomaly. In some cases, privately operated camera networks found in malls, sporting venues, and banks are being linked to community networks accessible to the police by means of memorandums of agreement or, if not normally accessible, have firewalls that can be quickly overridden under specific emergency guidelines.

Terrorist simulations now need to be conducted that leverage these sensor networks in real time as virtual support for counterterrorism operations. This has already been done with archived information with venue and local terrain mapping of two (x, y) and three (x, y, z) dimensional technology initiatives for both counterterrorism and active-shooter response training on the West Coast and in other parts of the United States.[7] The need now is to conduct dedicated simulations using both community sensor networks and integrating these real-time networks with archived technology initiatives to achieve more-comprehensive actionable operational intelligence. This will immediately benefit local response capabilities both by speeding up their OODA Loops and by ensuring that an OPFOR either does not obtain relative superiority or loses it quickly.

Terrorist Groups Organized as Networks

Very few if any simulations are specifically looking at netwar concepts and applying them to counterterrorism training and exercises.[8] This oversight needs to be rectified as more terrorist groups shift from hierarchical to networked organizational forms. This form of network-based conflict, or "netwar," is defined as "the lower-intensity, societal-level counterpart to our earlier, mostly military concept of cyberwar. . . . It is composed of conflicts waged, on the one hand, by terrorists, criminals, and ethnonationalist extremists; and by civil-society activists on the other. What distinguishes netwar as a form of conflict is the networked organizational structure of its practitioners—with many groups actually being leaderless—and the suppleness in their ability to come together quickly in swarming attacks."[9]

Basic network building blocks are viewed as chain, star, and all-channel networks, each with its own informational, offensive, and defensive strengths and weaknesses. In addition, no-channel networks (that is, nodes with no linkages) based on affinity and network-vision principles must also be considered as a new network type. Generally, smugglers use chain, organized terrorists use star, network-vision-based terrorists use no-channel, and anarchists use all-channel networks, but numerous exceptions to this typology exist. For terrorist simulation purposes, scenarios must be considered that focus on the organizational structure of the group itself and/or the operational expression of that structural form in such behaviors as "swarming" or "random nodal-generated attacks." Scenarios focused on organizational structure would primarily be intelligence-driven and preemptive simulations. A scenario in which the information processes of a star network attempting to acquire and utilize a weapon of mass destruction are being investigated would be one example. In contrast, behavior-based scenarios would focus on tactical teams and thus fall into transincident response. An example of such a scenario would be how to neutralize swarms of active aggressors who have converged on a targeted facility from all sides.

The need for these types of simulations has already been made apparent with the swarming tactics utilized by anarchists during the Battle for Seattle in 1999 and in many other protests, as well as with the continuing evolution of some groups of anarchists away from illicit and illegal street protests into quasi- and actual forms of terrorist activity. Other threat groups, including radical Islamic terrorists and insurgents and right-wing extremists, have for some time now been actively looking to network organizational forms as a defensive measure against group penetration by U.S. government agents, allied intelligence operatives, and paid or coerced informers. Such thinking was made widely known in 1992 with the publication of Louis Beam's concept of leaderless resistance in *The Seditionist* and eventual postings on the Web. These were derived from the earlier ideas of Ulius Amoss and have been gaining momentum with the emergence of extremist no-channel networks.

Private Security Forces and Mercenaries

There will be new "players" involved both as hostiles and as allies in future acts of terrorism. They must be factored in as participants in new simulations, as responders, and as red team members to test the ability of the authorities to both utilize and defend against them. The need to simulate these actors was touched upon earlier in the discussion of technicians with arcane knowledge of advanced and exotic weaponry. These individuals, however, represent only a small part of the actual changes now taking place in the global security environment with regard to new players and terrorism. Notably, corporate and private security forces have come back to the battlefield and homeland security environments—both foreign and domestic—with a vengeance, wielding an influence that had not been seen since the time of the High Middle Ages and the Renaissance.

While some of these groups will always be loyal to democratic governments, others will sell their talents to the highest bidder. Still others—because of their extreme religious or ideological views—will always be allied to terrorists and other threat groups. These new players will be significant in the pre- and transincident phases of the allied forces and significant in the planning, preparation, and execution phases of the opposing forces. In foreign areas of operation, such groups may be equivalent to Executive Outcomes and Blackwater levels of sophistication, meaning that they may be similar to elite U.S.

military units in their capabilities. This is significant because such groups (with members drawn, for example, from former Russian, American, and other elite military personnel) can have a positive significant operational impact for whomever they are contracted. This phenomenon has recently been witnessed with Los Zetas, former elite Mexican military personnel, who initially fought for the Gulf cartel. We must also remember that Hezbollah was stood up specifically in 1982 as a counter to the Israeli Defense Forces that were occupying southern Lebanon. Hezbollah originated with 1,500 members of the Iranian Revolutionary Guard being sent to southern Lebanon to help establish that terrorist group in coordination with the local Shia population.[10]

In domestic operations, Blackwater (now Xe) personnel were deployed in New Orleans during the aftermath of Katrina to protect affluent neighborhoods from looting and civil strife. The deployment of such groups in an allied counterterrorism role or as an actual terrorist strike force (composed of, say, former Russian Spetsnaz members working on behalf of a mafia, cartel, or terrorist organization) is no longer beyond the realm of pure fantasy. Already Los Zetas and similar cartel operatives are conducting low-profile operations within the United States and personnel belonging to other terrorist groups—some undoubtedly with specialized military skills—have traveled and will continue to travel freely throughout North America and Western Europe. Concern also exists that terrorist groups may stand up entirely new units drawn from former military personnel trained in such skills as strategic and futures planning, psychological operations, and electronic warfare to provide them with additional military-like capabilities that had not been possessed previously.

Ethnic, Linguistic, and Cultural Diversity

Globally, we now face terrorist groups that are increasingly diverse in ethnicity, language, and cultural backgrounds. As a response to this trend, the effective conduct of simulations will increasingly require a broader recruitment of personnel approximating the terrorist groups in question and those with specific cross-cultural expertise. This is imperative if we are to better know and understand our enemies. In particular, red team members should be a diverse mix and not those normally drawn from active U.S. law enforcement and military personnel (as was made very clear in chapter 5). Not surprisingly, the U.S. military has been increasing its use of anthropologists overseas and is actively promoting the "integration of cultural social sciences into its training and operations."[11] On domestic U.S. bases, we are also seeing the construction of Arab and Afghani villages populated with vetted foreign nationals for stability and support operations (SASO) training purposes. Red teams formed from those populations are the real deal minus the hostile intent and, if properly trained, are about as good as it gets short of using reformed terrorists—which is not going to happen because of OPSEC issues. From the response team side, having anthropologists and others who can address cross-cultural behaviors and associated dynamics during an exercise is invaluable. Knowledge of subtle body clues, hand gestures, and stances of a foreign nationals during negotiations is extremely important, as is the ability to listen in and understand unsecured communications in ethnic dialects.

One of Bunker's former graduate students is an African American male raised in the Nation of Islam until his late teen years before renouncing its doctrines. Much of this individual's research and observations have been unique and insightful because they are derived from the disenfranchised ethnic and cultlike experiences he grew up with. As a result, he was requested to help debrief the officers (specifically, the negotiators) who primarily dealt with the Beltway sniper shootings, due to his ability to get into the psyches of John Allen Muhammad and Lee Boyd Malvo. This is just one example of the real-world benefits that can be provided by utilizing diverse personnel.

Long-Term Community Disruption and Protection

A final recommendation is that after the standard postsimulation evaluation there needs to be a further series of activities to simulate the longer-term impact on those in the community who participated in or were indirectly affected by a terrorist simulation. This would include the responding forces and decision makers. This perspective transcends the preincident (interdiction), response, and consequence management phases gone through by the local responders. It helps to partially elevate the simulation of terrorist activity to higher strategic and political concerns that will influence a community's long-term mental and physical health. Hence, instead of operationally focused consequence management, we are promoting a form of strategically focused consequence management or community protection (akin to the military concept of force protection).

The reason for this perspective is that terrorism ultimately represents a form of disruptive targeting. It attacks the bonds and relationships that hold communities together. This is why a series of terrorist incidents can eventually erode and break apart community cohesiveness and well-being. It is also why failed terrorist attacks can be considered a success from the perspective of the threat group initiating them, since merely launching a failed attack on a community guarantees that high levels of disruptive effects will be unleashed upon it. Both authors have been involved in numerous terrorism-related exercises and simulations; we agree that, to this day, public information officers (PIOs) are typically the most underappreciated and underutilized members of the responding forces. This and similar issues are even now more significant because the "shelf life" of terrorist attacks will become longer due both to the increased capability of the terrorists to engage in more-lethal and mass acts of violence and destruction and to the impact that alternative forms of mass and discrete communication are now having on the perceptions of broad populations and targeted audiences. We are getting to the point that when a terrorist act is undertaken, those individuals and organizations identified as interested parties by means of associative databases and related information technologies are repeatedly alerted to the fact that it has taken place. The affected "community" thus must be broadened beyond the distinct geographic community involved with a terrorist act to all those contextually related to it.

THE ULTIMATE PURPOSE OF SIMULATIONS

We are deeply aware of the concern for developing simulation techniques that will not enable those countering terrorism not only to respond to but also to take the initiative against those who will continue to refine their capabilities against human and physical targets with murderous efficiency. We recognize that modern computer technology, new modes of communication and organization, and advanced weaponry place new requirements on those who wish to effectively develop simulations that will out-innovate the terrorists. But we also recognize that there are limits to what technology can do to enhance simulations. Other than being in that situation on the ground, there is no substitute for a sleep-deprived chief or colonel having to make a life-or-death decision at two in the morning; a sniper who has been on point for hours on hard, cold, wintry ground; a negotiator whose voice has cracked after long periods of frustrating discussion with a perpetrator; or a hostage who wonders about his or her faith as minutes turn to hours and hours to days. In their ultimate form, simulations are not virtual; they are the sum total of the experience, fear, and hopes of those who must be prepared to deal with the obscene reality of terrorism. The simulations must therefore ultimately test the interface between technology and the human-intensive activity of responding to an incident as well as the ability of senior decision makers who would ultimately be responsible for meeting the challenges. Finally, the simulations should involve stakeholders from the community on the state and local levels, for how they behave during and after the terrorist assault will largely determine the success or failure of those who have declared a war against all.

INTELLIGENCE-DRIVEN SIMULATIONS

As noted earlier, the role of intelligence has increased since *Simulating Terrorism* was written. The commitment of terrorists and active shooters to immediately killing their victims without negotiation and the increased availability of weapons of mass destruction have enhanced the requirement for proactive measures: no matter how effective first responders may be, they will often be primarily involved in damage control at a minimum and triage at the worst. Intelligence, therefore, is at the forefront of combating terrorism and other forms of premeditated violence by seeking out threats and preventing them from happening. Nevertheless, however good intelligence may be, some threats will be transformed into acts. Here, too, intelligence remains vital—in effectively responding to an incident. Ideally, a simulation should as much as possible test the capacity to identify threats before they take place (but also, if feasible, take effective action when they do occur). Although the focus in many simulations is on tactical and emergency management response, future exercises must incorporate the intelligence function as a major aspect of evaluating an organization's capability to respond to terrorism.

This appendix does not address all aspects of the intelligence process or provide a laundry list of different approaches that should be considered for each incident. Rather, it is generic, to be modified to assist in the development, conduct, and evaluation of simulations since, ultimately, each incident has its own unique dynamics. Three aspects of the intelligence process should be incorporated into the conducting of a simulation: (1) the collection and analysis of information, (2) the dissemination and integration of information, and (3) the decision-making process.

THE COLLECTION AND ANALYSIS OF INFORMATION: CREATING THE THREAT ENVIRONMENT

Incidents of terrorism do not take place in a vacuum. Many factors determine where, how, and why the terrorists will strike. As a result, authorities must develop the capability to identify potential incidents and take appropriate measures to prevent them. One of the major requirements necessary to achieve these goals is to acquire information and analyze it to assess the possibility of an attack. This is certainly a difficult task given the clandestine nature of various groups. Moreover, the difficulty behind acquisition of actionable data is exacerbated by the fact that when it is available it is often incomplete and difficult to analyze or is hidden in a plethora of information, with the "signal" that may warn of an attack thereby being masked by "noise." Any organization considering conducting a simulation should, therefore, consider having incorporated into the exercise a presimulation intelligence evaluation. This evaluation can help to test whether the jurisdictions in the impacted area have developed some capability to effectively collect data and analytically transform it into meaningful information that can be acted upon—ideally, to prevent an attack.

The requirement to know the threat environment can be refined by the red team by its providing some information, however limited, that can be input into the intelligence collection capabilities and files of the affected organization. This will help ascertain whether the organization has the ability to collect and analyze information that may serve as indications and warnings (I&W) of a terrorist campaign or act. The director of the simulation can add additional information to test the responding forces' intelligence capabilities. Certainly, there will be quite a difference between the intelligence capability of a large urban department and that of a small rural jurisdiction. Because ultimately "all terrorism is local," however, a vigilant small jurisdiction whose officers are aware of what is transpiring in their area of responsibilities through training can practice counterterrorism intelligence on the ground as an aspect of classic police intelligence. Given that a New Jersey State Police officer stopped a driver who was acting strangely on his way to bomb an economic summit meeting in Canada, a Border Patrol officer effectively stopped an individual from entering the United States to carry out an attack on the Los Angeles International Airport, and a county sheriff identified a white supremacist camp, clearly one person can make a difference, regardless of whether he or she is part of a large or small law enforcement organization. While the art and science of counterterrorism collection and analysis are complex, the basic principles of focus and awareness in meeting, analyzing, and countering a danger can be taught and tested through effective presimulation intelligence activities.

DISSEMINATION AND INTEGRATION OF INFORMATION: THE "I'VE GOT A SECRET" SYNDROME

Ultimately, no matter how sophisticated or substantive counterterrorism information may be, it is of little value if it is not disseminated to those organizations on all levels that are responsible for preventing or responding to terrorist acts. Tragically, the events of 9/11 underscored how the lack of cooperation among agencies helped set in motion the ability of the terrorists to carry out their attacks. Since that time, there have been positive developments with the creation of state, local, and national partnerships through counterterrorism task forces and fusion centers. But even then, the charges remain that the state and local forces are junior partners in these federally funded organizations and that the Federal Bureau of Investigation in particular takes far more information from the local level than it gives. In Sloan's state, the governor at one time did not have access to significant intelligence information because he did not have the necessary clearance. Fortunately, that has changed. The justification for this reluctance to share knowledge is often stated in terms of the need for classification to prevent information from being compromised or revealing sensitive sources and methods as to how it is acquired. It is, unfortunately, also a manifestation of the reality that each intelligence organization has its own culture and seeks a monopoly on various types of information in a so-called intelligence community where knowledge equals bureaucratic power. There have been positive developments, but there is a long way to go, for intelligence does not have meaning if it is not actionable to all the organizations that are involved in preventing or responding to terrorist threats.

THE DECISION-MAKING PROCESS: WHO'S IN CHARGE AND THE NEED FOR UNITY OF ACTION

Ultimately, one of the major objectives of a simulation (and that part of it driven by intelligence) will be to test the decision-making process and judgments made by those responsible for dealing with a threat or incident. The focus on intelligence will help to ascertain whether the decision makers are given the necessary information and the analysts have provided the appropriate knowledge to assist the senior officials in charge in taking the appropriate courses of action. The testing of the intelligence process will be complicated, given the stress involved in addressing a situation, particularly at the inception, when there will be little if any actionable intelligence. Moreover, whether the determination is made that immediate action should be initiated or whether negotiations are possible, as an incident develops the requirement for hard, on-the-ground specific tactical intelligence will be intensified. Such information as the number of perpetrators and hostages, the size and number of exit doors, the placement of the ventilation system, and similar facts may mean the difference between life and death when there is a tactical assault. This process can be further complicated if one is dealing with a multijurisdictional situation, in which the possibilities of bureaucratic and personality-driven turf battles can act as a barrier to a vital integration of effort. Further, even if one department clearly has the lead, the decision makers within it can also have their own disagreements. While one would like to think that in a crisis all the authorities are "reading from the same script," there have been and will continue to be disagreements when under the gun, as witnessed by conflicts between the ATF and FBI in the Branch Davidian siege and attack and the events of 9/11. As with all elements of dealing with terrorist attacks, it is important to test the ability within an individual agency and/or between numerous agencies to share the necessary information as they seek to resolve a critical incident. This will be particularly difficult given the high level of media coverage and the personal, community, and political demands that are faced by those who must handle a particular crisis, be it an active shooting in a school or a full-scale terrorist assault at a highly visible public location.

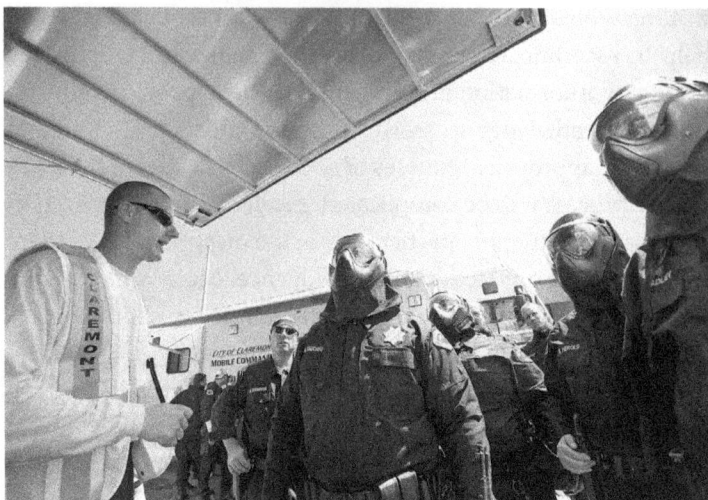

Active-shooter response mission briefing to Claremont Police officers prior to contact team movement into a courtyard leading to high school classrooms to begin the scenario. Single-agency response is much easier to manage and coordinate from a decision-making perspective. This briefing, prior to an active-shooting scenario, is provided to officers who are from a small law enforcement agency and are used to working with one another. As the size of an incident increases, the flow of timely and actionable intelligence to supporting agency personnel from other jurisdictions, and even bureaucratic turf battles, can become problematic. Courtesy of Gabriel Fenoy, *The Claremont Courier.*

MAJOR REQUIREMENT FOR AN
INTELLIGENCE-DRIVEN SIMULATION

In integrating into a simulation the key role of the intelligence function, the following elements can help guide the planners of such exercises:

Prior to the simulation, the simulation director should select an individual or individuals from the participating department(s) to act as liaison between him- or herself and the department in regard to the intelligence function. This individual should be a trusted agent who will share information only with the director. The intelligence liaison should first require the department or departments to use their own sources of information and the networks they may be connected to in order to engage in a general threat assessment as it relates to their jurisdiction. This will not only test the interoperability of intelligence sources but also give the analyst an opportunity to develop and present his or her assessment to the department(s).

As the simulation develops, the simulation director will provide information in regard to the potential threat that will occur during the simulation. The material will be based on his own analysis of the simulated threat, and he should also get fragmentary information from the red cell in regard to their planned operation. This information should be kept between him and the cell.

The simulation director should then provide this information to the intelligence liaison, who, if possible, should input the fragmentary information into the available databases and other sources. If this is not possible, the intelligence liaison should have at least three computers representing different sources of intelligence information and input selective data on each of them. The object of this exercise will be to test the ability of the department to acquire available information and test the ability of the analyst to separate the "noise from the signal" related to potential attacks. Again, the information must be fragmentary and, at times, contradictory.

When the simulation begins, additional information will be provided by the liaison to the department(s). Further intelligence can be input on the computer or passed by phone, by texting, by e-mail, and/or verbally by various sources as the exercise progresses.

As the simulation continues, more-detailed information—both correct and erroneous—will be passed, much of it tactical in nature and actionable. The decision makers will need to determine whether they want to use this information in conducting counterterrorism operations involved in hostage rescues or killing and capturing the terrorists as well as other objectives.

After the simulation is over, an initial evaluation of the intelligence process should be conducted based on a log and documents maintained by the intelligence liaison.

The information from the intelligence process should continually be updated to reflect the changing dynamics of the simulated incident. The key to the intelligence-driven simulation is to evaluate whether the information has been disseminated, whether the analyst gave good assessments, and not only whether the decision makers received the information but also whether they chose to use it. One point that should be kept in mind is that intelligence has a key role in regard to both prevention and response. The intelligence function does not represent a support mission but is instead a major aspect of any negotiative or tactical response.

Hostage-Taking and Active-Aggressor Simulations

The conduct of terrorism has dramatically changed since Brian Jenkins's much quoted 1970s observation, "Terrorists want a lot of people watching and a lot of people listening and not a lot of people dead."[1] The shift by terrorists to the immediate killing of innocents on sight, the taking of hostages and their subsequent torture and execution, and a general willingness to now engage in mass killing is the primary reason why the need for intelligence-driven simulations is highlighted in appendix 1. Such simulations allow for the facilitation of proactive counterterrorism operations. Hand in hand with this need for better intelligence training comes the need to determine how to respond to an actual incident involving active aggressors who have gained entry to a facility and/or have taken over parts of it, along with taking hostages. The archetype of this type of terrorist incident is the Beslan school takeover in Russia in September 2004. This represents a high-end incident involving trained Chechen terrorists heavily armed with military small arms, body armor, and suicide vests and the extensive use of IEDs deployed in the barricaded venue. Midlevel incidents are on the level of the Columbine massacre in April 1999, with a couple of active shooters having plenty of arms and ammunition but whose use of IEDs and general tactics were far more amateurish and unprofessional in nature. Low-end incidents represent basic active-shooter situations in which an individual brings a firearm to a school or other venue and simply opens fire on those around him, with or without some sort of basic ops plan. Mixed in with these more ominous scenarios are the older types of situations in which individual and multiple hostages are taken by slightly deranged individuals and less ideologically violent groups who want to make a public statement but are less committed to mass homicide and may be willing to reach a negotiated settlement to the crisis they have created.

This appendix is not able to cover all response variants to hostage-taking and active-aggressor incidents. Huge variations in response between urban and rural police departments are also evident, along with the willingness of a department to send a lone officer directly into a venue while gunfire is taking place. Four aspects of hostage-taking and active-aggressor incidents should be considered when conducting simulations: (1) the initial assessment, (2) negotiation approaches, (3) tactical assault approaches, and (4) a combination approach.

MAKING THE INITIAL ASSESSMENT: TO TALK OR TO SHOOT

No definitive national or state guidelines exist concerning how to initially determine whether a hostage takeover or an active-aggressor incident is taking place. The outcome of such an assessment will determine whether response forces should initially talk or shoot. What guidelines exist are still emerging from police associations and individual departments or are provided by contractors providing tactical response training. What is now accepted is that the old contain-and-wait strategy is no longer viable in this age of increased violence and the threat of terrorism. Always creating a perimeter and blindly adopting a wait-and-see or a wait-for-SWAT mentality has now been discredited because of the tragic loss of life it has caused to those who otherwise might have been rescued early on or been provided life-saving medical attention for their injuries.

Any organization considering conducting this type of simulation need now consider undertaking a presimulation evaluation of the ability of patrol and supervisory personnel first arriving on the scene to make a hasty tactical assessment of the type of incident that they are responding to. This assessment process needs to have some sort of simple criteria for deadly force to be immediately employed, such as, Will the use of deadly force save those imperiled from the imminent threat of bodily injury or death? To help make the initial assessment whether to engage the threat force or shift over to negotiations, two forms of information should be utilized: one drawn from accounts and information provided by witnesses to the incident, the second drawn from information personally obtained by the responding officers. The first means of gaining information will be hastily derived from HUMINT (human intelligence) provided by witnesses at the scene of the incident to the responding officer or officers. Eyewitness accounts of people being shot or lying on the floor bleeding will have a large impact on the responding officers' assessment of the situation. Dispatchers can also provide this information originating from witnesses still trapped inside the targeted venue to responding officers. The responding officers represent the second means of gaining information. The sounds of gunshots and screams heard by the responding officers or images of wounded victims on the ground or running away from the scene will have an immediate impact on incident response. While video camera images of the venue would represent another means of gaining intelligence, and the information should be utilized if applicable, these systems are still normally not a local law enforcement resource.

The above means of gaining information will help the responding officers quickly attempt to place the incident into context and determine opposing force (OPFOR) intent, that is, is it

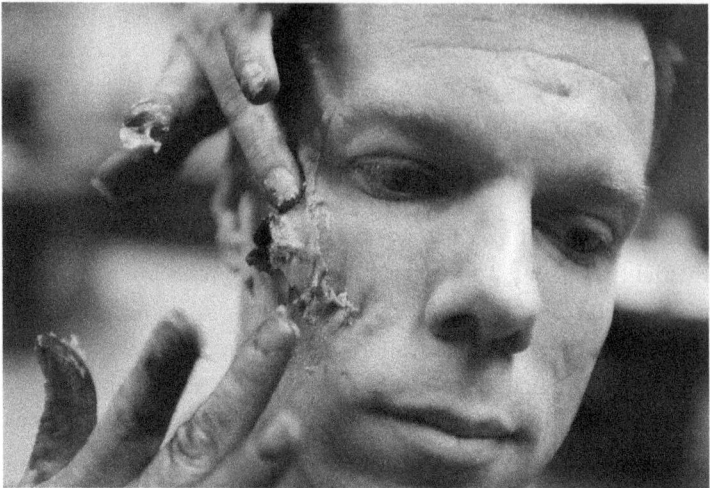

Active-shooter exercises are becoming more realistic as injuries are being better simulated. The photograph shows U.S. Air Force Major Brian Ignotowicz, chief of the plans division with the Twenty-eighth Bomb Wing, sitting as moulage is placed on him to simulate an injury before the beginning of an active-shooter exercise on April 15, 2010, at Ellsworth Air Force Base, South Dakota. Courtesy of U.S. Air Force, photo by Senior Airman Adam Grant (released).

an active-shooter incident, a hostage incident, or a terrorist assault? The final validation will come with the initial responding officers moving forward and making contact with the suspect or threat group, making an entry if necessary.[2] Contact has to be made quickly because of relative superiority and operational tempo concerns of ceding the advantage to the threat group. Once this contact is made, the responding officers will be at a decision point and will either tactically engage the OPFOR, if they have achieved surprise and have not been already fired upon, or take up forward defensive positions and approach this as a hostage situation. In the latter instance, follow-on forces would create an outer restrictive perimeter and establish a command post, triage, staging, and debriefing areas. A hostage negotiation team would be brought into the incident, dedicated contact and rescue teams formed, and snipers positioned for use as the incident response further dictates. Secondary device sweeps of the staging areas and immediate choke points and the use of countersurveillance protocols, even if only hastily conducted initially, should also be undertaken.

Making the initial decision to take a negotiation or tactical assault approach, however, does not mean that the incident is static and cannot change rapidly. Additional decision points will potentially exist for responding officers with regard to the response continuum approaches at their disposal.

NEGOTIATION APPROACHES

Unlike when *Simulating Terrorism* was published, most law enforcement agencies and departments now have trained negotiators who, at the very least, have learned the basic principles of negotiation. The art of negotiation has certainly evolved over the years, and the requirement for negotiators will remain (whether dealing with a domestic disturbance, a barricade hostage situation, an active aggressor, or a full-blown terrorist incident). But some guidance must be considered.

As in the case of a tactical situation, there may not be time to wait for either a trained SWAT team or a hostage negotiation team. The first responders may have to take on these roles, at least at the inception of an incident, and therefore must be given a level of training that can enable them to do so until specialized units can be involved (assuming that such units are available). The tasks may be very daunting; while aware of their limitations, the first responders must take action, for as noted earlier, time will not be on the side of the authorities.

There has been and increasingly continues to be the need for both hostage negotiators and tactical teams to understand their respective missions. The negotiation team must understand when they must hand over the operation to the tactical team even if there has been a long and at times positive negotiation, and the tactical team must not act hastily due to frustration if negotiation appears to still be a viable option. The key is that, while their tasks and mindsets may be different based on their training and duties, each must keep in mind that ultimately they are on the same team. It is vital that the respective specialists do not act at cross purposes.

As noted in chapter 14 of *Simulating Terrorism* (entitled "You Can't Negotiate by the Numbers"), the negotiators, irrespective of level of training, must maintain a degree of flexibility and objectivity in carrying out their responsibilities. This will be no easy task, but a beat officer with no specialized training along with others at various levels of training would all benefit from their involvement in a simulation. The fact is that there is no guarantee that one will have the time or expertise that one would desire at the inception of a crisis.

Finally, as a guideline, in the case of a multijurisdictional situation, the first responding department should initially be in charge. Any handover based on jurisdiction and level of training should be done smoothly. There is little room for "jurisdictional gridlock" in the midst of an active-aggressor or hostage situation. Simulations can be used to achieve the necessary unity of action, provided that the various agencies are all willing to take part.

TACTICAL ASSAULT APPROACHES

A wide range of initial tactical approaches to responding to an active-shooter or active-aggressor incident currently exist. These approaches basically trade response speed and operational tempo (optempo) for officer safety and the massing of forces against the suspect or threat force. Rural jurisdictions will typically send in a lone officer to respond to an incident because backup forces will not exist within the immediate area and may be tens of miles away. Suburban and urban departments have numerous responding officers who can be on the scene within minutes, and typically a four-man contact team will be hastily created and will seek to gain entry into the incident site and make contact with the opposing force. Typically, this force will be tightly bunched up and move slowly forward in a diamond formation, in a T-formation (with three men on line and one behind), or in a Y-formation (so that corner ambushes in hallway settings are minimized by removing the vulnerable point man position). This general approach is well suited to neutralize one or two unsophisticated active shooters, with the more sophisticated contact teams shifting formations as the terrain and threat level changes. Criticisms of this approach are that it is slow in its response and that the bunching up of officers will create a large target set, which is vulnerable to IED and assault-weapon-based kill zones set up by more-sophisticated threats and terrorists. Proposals for more-military-like two-man contact teams that are quickly assembled, use a wider formation, and provide fire-and-maneuver-support represent one method to overcome this vulnerability. Just recently, in the spring of 2010, a shift to single-officer response to active shooters in suburban and urban settings has also begun to be debated in some tactical policing circles. For simulation purposes, quite a bit of thought should be focused on departmental response capabilities—personnel, equipment, and training—and likely threats to determine appropriate tactical assault approaches that should be utilized. More-advanced active-shooter response programs will include the use of multiple contact teams and immediate follow-on response teams to stabilize and transport the wounded. The inclusion of combat-medics—police officers who are armed but can also render forward medical aid to injured contact team members and shooting victims—is also being discussed and can be readily simulated for scenario purposes.

COMBINED APPROACH

Any simulation that does not end quickly in an initial and successful tactical assault against active shooters will have the potential for responding forces to ultimately utilize a combined approach to solve the incident. This approach will draw upon both negotiation (good cop) and tactical assault (bad cop) approaches and seeks to create synergies between them. This approach may provide enhanced negotiation opportunities by moving tactical forces from overt to covert positions as a sign of de-escalation or the reverse, as in the escalation of force, with the overt movements of a tactical unit, such as an armored personnel carrier (APC), to show the futility of further resistance. This approach may also provide enhanced assault opportunities by using negotiations as a ruse to enable sensing equipment (such as microphones or mini cameras) to be covertly brought into the barricaded facility, create situations where clear sniper shots can be taken, or even provide the opening needed for the contact force to make entry and neutralize the threat.

MAJOR REQUIREMENTS FOR
A HOSTAGE-TAKING AND
ACTIVE-AGGRESSOR SIMULATION

In injecting into simulations the appropriate challenges and training for active assaults, hostage taking, and more-complex incidents, the following elements can help guide the planners of such response exercises:

1. Prior to the simulation, the simulation director should select an individual or individuals from the participating department(s) to act as liaison between himself and the department with regard to the hostage-taking and active-shooter training. This individual should be

a trusted agent who will share information only with the director. The hostage and active-aggressor liaison should first require the department(s) to determine the assessment criteria used by their patrol and supervisory personnel when responding to these incidents in order to engage in a response assessment as it relates to their jurisdiction. This will not only gauge the jurisdiction's response protocols but also give the training officer an opportunity to develop and present his or her assessment to the department(s) with regard to simulation training needs.

2. Basic forms of training should initially be provided focusing on discrete active-shooter (aggressor) and hostage-taking response. A key focus of this training will be on the tactical assessment process utilized by the responding officers as they make contact with the threat group. The key learning point is how the responding officers utilize eyewitness information (HUMINT) and the information they gain on-scene to quickly put the incident into context and determine intent upon contact with the opposing force.

3. As the simulation develops, the simulation director will provide information with regard to the potential threat that will occur during the simulation. The material will be based on his own analysis of the simulated threat, and he should also get fragmentary information from the red cell in regard to their planned operation. This information should be kept between him and the cell.

4. When the simulation begins, more-detailed information—both correct and erroneous—will be passed, almost all of it tactical in nature and actionable. It will be up to the initial responding officers (and, if applicable, follow-on decision makers) to determine how they want to utilize this information.

5. As the simulation progresses, further intelligence can be input on the computer or passed by phone, by texting, by e-mail, and/or verbally by various sources. In an active-shooter simulation, this stage will typically be skipped, while in more-drawn-out hostage-taking and barricade scenarios this information can provide insight into why individual suspect and/or threat group actions are taking place.

6. After the simulation is over, an initial and immediate evaluation (hot wash) of the response should be conducted with those who participated in the exercise.

The most challenging response simulations will be based on a complex threat that incorporates elements of both an active-shooter incident and a traditional hostage taking in an ongoing and dynamic situation. This will require the responding forces to quickly shift their operational style and approach to meet the demands of the simulation. The actual length, difficulty, and focus of the simulation will be dependent on local training needs and can range from basic active-shooter scenarios all the way through Beslan-like (a large-scale armed school takeover) and Mumbai-type (citywide multiple armed assaults and barricade) terrorist incidents.

THE COST OF FAILURES IN INTELLIGENCE

The Tragedy of Fort Hood

The recent Fort Hood tragedy is illustrative of the critical need for actionable intelligence so that active-aggressor incidents can be preempted before anyone is killed or injured. Still, intelligence exists in numerous forms and at various levels. With regard to this incident, three forms of intelligence can be identified via the information currently available: strategic, preincident, and transincident intelligence.

FORMS OF INTELLIGENCE

Strategic Intelligence

Given recent trends concerning active-aggressor incidents, this form of intelligence readily existed pertaining to the overall basic threat environment. This threat was well understood by base security personnel as well as by members of local law enforcement agencies. That such a threat existed was further driven home by the Luby's Cafeteria incident that took place in nearby Killeen, Texas, in 1991. In that incident, twenty-three people were shot to death and twenty people wounded in a fourteen-minute shooting spree that ended only after the shooter took his own life. The radicalization of some Islamic adherents, both within and outside of the U.S. military, and their subsequent willingness to engage in acts of violence had also been noted as a potentiality. Additionally, the inter-relationship of these individuals to mental illness had been discussed and analyzed on numerous occasions. These basic threat environment facts thus were well known to local security and police forces.

Pre-incident Intelligence

This form of intelligence is centered on the behaviors, mannerisms, and actions of the active aggressor, Major Nidal Hasan, leading up to the tragedy at Fort Hood. This is where actionable intelligence would have proved its value and averted the death and injury of so many. It would have required the linking of Hasan's actions and activities within the larger context of the threat identified by the preexisting strategic intelligence—active-aggressor incidents, the radicalization of some Islamic adherents and their subsequent willingness to engage in acts of violence, and the overlap between—which was not done. Why and how these linkages were not made is still unknown, though initial observations and insights are provided in the second half of this appendix. Lessons learned from this incident will have great value for future simulation exercises and, we hope, will someday be applied by some of the readers.

Transincident Intelligence

This form of intelligence, tactical in nature, and is concerned solely with the Fort Hood incident while it was in progress. Such intelligence is hasty in nature, is based in the immediate threat, and focuses on basics such as who, what, why, where, how, and when. Two civilian police officers from different agencies responded independently to the shooting, apparently at the same time; they linked up and then engaged Major Hasan as he was still in the process of gunning down individuals fleeing into an exterior area outside of the main shooting scene. Current estimates are that this response came about ten minutes after the incident had begun. The individual actions of these officers slowed Hasan down and ultimately allowed for his neutralization and arrest. Of note is that these officers responded utilizing the proposed military contact team method (see appendix 2)—engage the active aggressor in a two-man team—rather than waiting to assault until a larger four-man contact team was assembled. In this instance, the hasty decision to go with speed of response and an ad hoc two-man team most probably saved numerous lives and injuries.

THE FORT HOOD INCIDENT

On November 5, 2009, Major Nidal Malik Hasan walked into the Readiness Center at Fort Hood, Texas, and started to fire indiscriminately at personnel preparing for assignments overseas in Afghanistan and Iraq. The tragic result was thirteen killed, twenty-nine wounded, and a base and its community (which had some members deployed worldwide) traumatized. The full details of what happened were subject to a congressional hearing by members of the Homeland Security Committee as well as to various investigations by the Pentagon and the intelligence community. More detailed information is to be disclosed in a report by the former head of the Federal Bureau of Investigation, William Webster, and will be released as the trial of Major Hasan commences.

As in the case of other incidents, it is too early to definitively judge why the incident took place and what could have been done to prevent it. But current accounts of what transpired

Intelligence failures can readily lead to domestic casualties and deaths. In the photo, a flag flies at half-mast during a memorial ceremony on Fort Hood, Texas, November 10, 2009. The ceremony was held to honor thirteen service members who were killed at the base's processing station on November 5, 2009. Courtesy DoD, photo by Cherie Cullen (released).

highlight the key role that pre-incident intelligence could have played in possibly preventing the tragedy. In the months to come, the "blame game" will be played as each agency and department seeks to distance itself from what appears at present to be a major failure of intelligence. There may, however, ultimately be enough culpability to go around as, on the face of it, the signals seem to have been there that Major Hasan was a ticking time bomb increasingly ready to engage in an act of carnage—be it called mass murder or terrorism or both. We recognize the benefit of hindsight, but even without a significant passage of time, we can seek to learn something from the events leading up to Fort Hood.

At the outset, there appear to have been acts of omission in the availability of important facts relating to Hasan; this underscores that information is no good if it is not effectively collected and analyzed. In the case of Major Hasan, there were numerous signals that he was becoming increasingly unhappy with his commitment to serve in the military and that over time his feelings began to take on a religious overtone, evidenced by his strong articulation that he did not want to fight against those who shared his basic faith.

He expressed these concerns as a medical student at the Uniformed Services University of Health Sciences. For example, at a seminar on environmental health, he gave a PowerPoint presentation entitled "Why the War on Terror Is a War on Islam." There are constraints on what can be done legally and politically in this context. How such a presentation relates to the topic of the seminar is highly questionable, but such a presentation, in and of itself, is an exercise of freedom of speech, particularly in an academic institution. Although in retrospect it appears a warning of things to come, it was not at that time a piece of information that could be identified and acted upon. There may have also been reluctance on the part of staff and students to verbalize their concern over Hasan's behavior because of the worry that they might appear to be biased. Of course, there were other warning signs, including the major's desire to leave the military despite his seven-year commitment to the army after finishing medical school. Especially troublesome is that Major Hasan had met with firebrand cleric Anwar al-Aulaqi when he attended a mosque in Falls Church, Virginia, and, moreover, that this association would continue over the Internet when the imam moved to Yemen. Al-Aulaqi continued distributing radical fundamentalist views not only to Hasan but also to a broader audience, and this relationship may have been one of the factors that potentially led to a radicalization process that culminated in the Fort Hood attack. Unfortunately, this information was not considered in a comprehensive connect-the-dots manner and did not trigger any alarm.

Especially vexing is that many of these Internet messages, which incidentally included the transfer of funds, were known by the FBI's Counterterrorism Task Force; the local FBI office in San Diego, where Hasan then lived, appeared not to have viewed the information as indicating a threat to national security. Perhaps alone it did not, but of particular concern is the fact that the information was evidently not shared with other federal, state, and local agencies that might have found the information valuable in raising their perception and awareness of a potential threat. Apparently, despite all the money and reorganization of the intelligence community in the name of homeland security, when information means political and economic power it still may not be shared, under the justification of being on a "need to know" basis.

In the final analysis, the Fort Hood tragedy serves to underscore that even good information is useless if it (1) is not disseminated to all those who need it and (2) is not actionable, that is, can be acted upon by those who have security and law enforcement responsibilities. Admittedly, charting a radicalization process, reconciling freedom of speech with security requirements, and achieving the unity of outlook and cooperation needed to counter terrorism and other forms of violence are all difficult. In this case, we are left with the painful "what if" questions that have been raised: What if the provost marshal on the base had some knowledge of Major Hasan's behavior and activities? What if the military and civilian guards therefore had a heightened level of vigilance? What if the local police were at least given sufficient information to more closely monitor the sale of weapons? There are many more "what ifs" that only reaffirm the vital role of intelligence in preventing rather than primarily responding to threats and acts of terrorism. What the final "lessons that should be learned" from Fort Hood will be remain to be seen. We only hope that such lessons can be learned, acted upon, and tested in simulations earlier rather than later, in the interest of prevention, so that they are not lamented in their absence after the future incidents that will take place in the weeks, months, or years to come.

NOTES

PREFACE

1. Rupert Emerson, *From Empire to Nation: The Rise to Self-Assertion of Asian and African People* (Cambridge, Mass.: Harvard University Press, 1960).

2. Stephen Sloan, *A Study in Political Violence: The Indonesian Experience* (Chicago: Rand McNally, 1971).

3. Ibid., 4.

4. Stephen Sloan, "The Functionality of Violence in the New States of Asia and Africa: A Reassessment of Developmental Theory," paper delivered at the Annual Meeting of the American Political Science Association, 1971.

5. Stephen Sloan, "Almost Present at the Creation: A Personal Perspective of a Continuing Journey," *Journal of Conflict Studies* 24, no. 1 (Summer 2004).

6. These full-scale simulations and command post exercises dealing with crisis management included simulations with the 416th Security Police Squadron, Griffiss Air Force Base, Rome, New York, June 19, 1986; the U.S. Commandant, Berlin, Commander Berlin Brigade, and the Berlin Crisis Management Team in conjunction with West German authorities, May 18–19, 1982; the 51st Security Police Squadron, Osan Air Force Base, Korea, September 5, 1980; the Special Operations Team, Tulsa Police Department in conjunction with the Sun Oil Refinery, Tulsa, Oklahoma, September 19, 1978; in conjunction with hostage negotiation course, New Zealand Police, Police College

Trentham, New Zealand, October 20, 1977; the 7th Special Operations Group (Airborne), Fort Gulick, Canal Zone, January 2, 1977; and as part of the International Conference on Terrorism, Norman Police Department, September 22, 1976.

7. Brian Jenkins, *New Modes of Conflict* (Santa Monica, Calif.: RAND, 1983).

8. For an interview regarding the Oklahoma City bombing, see "Is U.S. Ripe for Terrorist Attacks?" *Daily Bulletin*, April 20, 1995, p. A4. For an early description of what one of these nonstate entities might look like, see Robert J. Bunker, *Five-Dimensional (Cyber) Warfighting: Can the Army after Next Be Defeated through Complex Concepts and Technologies?* (Carlisle Barracks, Penn.: U.S. Army War College, Strategic Studies Institute, March 10, 1998).

9. For red teaming and response purposes, the following training keys are extremely useful: Robert J. Bunker, *Laser Threats to Law Enforcement*, Training Key no. 523 (Alexandria, Va.: International Association of Chiefs of Police, November 2000) and *Suicide (Homicide) Bombers*, Training Key nos. 581 and 582 (Alexandria, Va.: International Association of Chiefs of Police, July 2005).

10. Robert J. Bunker, "Street Gangs: Future Paramilitary Groups?" *Police Chief* (June 1996): 54–59.

11. Stephen Sloan, *Terrorism: The Present Threat in Context* (Oxford, U.K.: Berg, 2006).

ORGANIZATION OF THE BOOK

Epigraph: A comment by a fellow professor who opposed Stephen Sloan's request to offer a course on international terrorism in 1975.

CHAPTER 1. TERRORISM AND SIMULATIONS TODAY

Epigraph: A statement attributed to Josephus, a first-century Jewish historian.

1. Stephen Sloan, "Almost Present at the Creation: A Personal Perspective of a Continuing Journey," *Journal of Conflict Studies* 24, no. 1 (Summer 2004).

2. Stephen Sloan and Richard Kearney, "Non-territorial Terrorism: An Empirical Approach to Policy Formulation," *Conflict: An International Journal for Conflict and Policy Studies* 1, no. 1–2 (1978).

3. Brian Jenkins, *New Modes of Conflict* (Santa Monica, Calif.: RAND, 1983).

4. Colonel Lloyd J. Matthews, ed., *Challenging the United States Symmetrically and Asymmetrically: Can America Be Defeated?* (Carlisle Barracks, Penn.: U.S. Army War College, Strategic Studies Institute, 1998).

5. Thomas Strentz, *Psychological Aspects of Crisis Negotiation* (Boca Raton, La.: Taylor and Francis, 2006), 219.

6. These high figures partly resulted from the lack of any other option, since negotiation had failed. Brian Jenkins, Janera Johnson, and David Ronfeldt, *Numbered Lives: Some Statistical Observations from 77 International Hostage Episodes* (Santa Monica, Calif.: RAND, 1972), 27.

7. Stephen Sloan, *Simulating Terrorism* (Norman: University of Oklahoma Press, 1981), 92–93.

8. See Robert J. Bunker, "Defending against the Non-state (Criminal) Soldier: Toward a Domestic Response Network," *Police Chief* 65, no. 11 (November 1998): 41–49.

9. Michael T. McEwen and Stephen Sloan, eds., "Terrorism, Police and Press Problems," *Terrorism: An International Journal* 1, no. 1–2 (1979).

10. Stephen Sloan, *Terrorism: The Present Threat in Context* (Oxford, UK: Berg, 2006), 109.

CHAPTER 2. BASIC PRINCIPLES OF CONDUCTING A SIMULATION

Epigraph: Sloan's experience in dealing with bureaucracy in conducting simulations.

1. In the computer security profession, reformed hackers have been employed in a red team role. This is probably because the illegality of their past actions is relatively light compared to the crimes committed by bona fide terrorists. See Kevin D. Mitnick and William L. Simon, *The Art of Deception: Controlling the Human Element of Security* (Indianapolis: Wiley, 2002); and Kevin D. Mitnick and William L. Simon, *The Art of Intrusion: The Real Stories behind the Exploits of Hackers, Intruders and Detectives* (Indianapolis: Wiley, 2005).

2. Sean D. Naylor, "War Games Rigged? General Says Millennium Challenge 02 'Was Almost Entirely Scripted,'" *Army Times*, August 16, 2002, http://www.armytimes.com/legacy/new/0-292925-1060102.php.

3. Stephen Sloan, "Meeting the Terrorist Threat: The Localization of Counterterrorism Intelligence," *Police Practices and Research* 3, no. 4 (December 2002).

4. Samuel M. Katz, *Jihad in Brooklyn: The NYPD Raid That Stopped America's First Suicide Bombers* (New York: New American Library, 2005).

5. For measures that can be used in promoting involvement in countering terrorism, see J. B. Hill and Joshua A. Smith, "Appendix: Working Through Terrorism at the Individual, Family and Community Level," in Stephen Sloan, *Terrorism: The Present Threat in Context* (Oxford, UK: Berg, 2006).

CHAPTER 3. GUIDING THE SIMULATION

Epigraph: Attributed to Helmuth von Moltke, who was a German field marshal and chief of staff of the Prussian Army in the nineteenth century.

1. In the Department of Homeland Security exercise planning process derived from the incident command system (defined in the National Incident Management System), safety, operations (site liaison, resources), planning (exercise documentation, evaluation), logistics (props, actors), and administration/finance (reporting, budgeting) components have to be covered. The danger always exists that simulation planning can morph from being a functional and streamlined endeavor to a ritualized and overly bureaucratic one because of federal involvement in the process.

2. "Letter of Instruction Format (LOI) / Fragmentary Order Format, I MEF FY-08 Campaign Plan" (Camp Pendleton, Calif.: United States Marine Corps, n.d.).

3. For a discussion on terrorist arms and associated equipment, see Sloan, *Simulating Terrorism*, 57–59.

4. Christopher M. Schnaubelt, "Lessons in Command and Control from the Los Angeles Riots," *Parameters* (Summer 1997): 88, quoted in James D. Delk, *Fires and Furies: The L.A. Riots* (Palm Springs, Calif.: ETC Publications, 1995), 221–22.

5. Sloan, *Simulating Terrorism*, 61–63.

CHAPTER 4. MURPHY'S LAW CAN PROVE FATAL

1. Concern also exists that fictitious reports of terrorist activity may be called into the emergency (911) system by actual operatives to observe law enforcement response times and procedures, command

post locations, and avenues of approach. Such knowledge of enemy capabilities and dispositions would be utilized by terrorist groups in their planning of an actual incident and would provide them the intelligence necessary to implement highly successful "kill zones" with secondary and tertiary devices.

2. Issues still exist today with the need to incorporate both criminal intelligence and military intelligence techniques in counterterrorism fusion cells. Law enforcement agencies, when left to their own devices, will fall into their comfort zones and focus on the criminal attributes of terrorism. This exclusion of military intelligence perspectives results in a capability gap developing with regard to understanding "enemy intent" and the "probable enemy courses of action," which is required for effectively responding to a terrorist campaign being launched against a local jurisdiction such as that of a large metropolitan area.

3. See Stephen Sloan, "Meeting the Terrorist Threat: The Localization of Counter Terrorism Intelligence" *Public Practice and Research* 3, no. 4 (2002); "Community Response to Terrorism," PowerPoint presentation under the auspices of the Oklahoma Sheriff's Association, the Oklahoma Association of Chiefs of Police, and the Oklahoma Regional Community Policing Institute (Oklahoma City, 2000). The importance of having a sense of community in the wake of a crisis came home to Sloan on a personal level when the British Broadcasting Corporation interviewed his daughter Maya, who was then a senior in high school and felt the loss of people she knew or knew of in the bombing of the Federal Building. She said there was a particularly strong sense of community loss, given the size of the city; to illustrate her point, she referred to the play and later movie *Six Degrees of Separation*, which used as a theme the belief that we are all related and only separated by at most six degrees. She said, "In Oklahoma City, we are separated by four degrees of separation." But that sense of shared loss has also been experienced in larger cities that have been subject to attack, such as New York, London, Madrid, Mumbai, and other locales that have experienced such attacks in the past and unfortunately in all probability will experience additional assaults in the future.

4. See "Noted Police Chief Slams Federal-Local Partnerships," *National Defense* (March 2009): 12.

5. From an offensive perspective, the use of a "'global counterterrorism network' made up of many small special operations teams scattered around the world working with partner nations to hunt down terrorists and insurgents" is increasingly being discussed. See

Greg Grant, "Irregular Warfare Shift Accelerating in QDR," Dodbuzz
.com, March 18, 2009.

6. Lieutenant Colonel David Bradford (USA, ret.), "The Shadow
Falls: The Gray Area Phenomenon in Today's World," unpublished
paper, 1995.

7. This is reminiscent of the 1997 film *Wag the Dog* (starring Robert
De Niro and Dustin Hoffman), in which a fake war with Albania was
created to take the spotlight off the U.S. president, who was involved
in a sex scandal.

8. Brian Jenkins, *International Terrorism: A New Mode of Conflict,*
California Seminar on Arms Control and Foreign Policy Research
Paper 48 (Los Angeles: Crescent Publication, 1975), 4.

CHAPTER 5. THE RED TEAM

Epigraph: An observation by Robert Bunker concerning a Mirror
Image course taken in Moyock, North Carolina, in September 2004.

1. See the discussion on criminal and OPFOR threat continuums
in Robert J. Bunker, "Adversary Weaponry to 2025," in *Policing and Future Social Dynamics: Potential Adversaries and Allies,* ed. Earl Moulton,
Futures Working Group 7 (Washington, D.C.: U.S. Department of Justice). Forthcoming.

2. "TRC Training Presents: Mirror Image: Training to Combat Terrorism," Terrorism Research Center Web site, http://www.terrorism.com.

3. Evan Wright, "Camp Jihad," *New York Magazine,* November 29,
2004, http://nymag.com/nymetro/news/features/10558/.

4. Brigadier General Joseph Anderson, "Out-of-the-Box Thinkers:
Red Teams Are Operating at the Corps Level in Iraq," *Armed Forces Journal,* November 2008, www.armedforcesjournal.com/2008/11/ 3759060.

5. Richard Marcinko, *Red Cell: The True Story* (Brentwood, Calif.:
L.O.T.I. Group Productions, 1994), VHS, color, 55 minutes.

6. Dave Grossman, "Autopilot," in Grossman, *On Combat* (Belleville, Ill.: PPCT Research Publications, 2004).

7. Personal correspondence with the Mirror Image cell leader on
January 27, 2009, by e-mail and telephone conversation.

8. "Mexican Cartels and the Fallout from Phoenix," *Stratfor,* July 2,
2008.

9. Differing perspectives on terrorist targeting strategies can be
found in Colonel Phil Harmon II (Marine Expeditionary Force Fwd

AT-FP red team leader) and Master Gunnery Sergeant David Franco (AT-FP special ops and red team chief), "Red Team Assessment Methodology" (unclassified slides). For Colonel G. I. Wilson (OIC MNF–West Iraq AT-FP, Camp Fallujah, Iraq, October 2005), that utilizes a CARVER targeting process and Peter Probst's red team models, which draw upon databases that terrorists would use to assess vulnerabilities, found in Joshua Sinai, "Red Teaming the Terrorist Threat to Preempt the Next Waves of Catastrophic Terrorism" (Arlington, Va.: ANSER, 2003), a PowerPoint presentation at the Fourteenth Annual NDIA SO/LIC Symposium and Exhibition, February 12, 2003.

10. Terrorists can be classified in various ways. A broader five-level classification based on their skill levels can be found in Malcolm W. Nance, *The Terrorist Recognition Handbook*, 2nd ed. (Boca Raton, Fla.: CRC Press, 2008), 14–25.

CHAPTER 6. GETTING THE RED TEAM
READY FOR ITS ROLE

Epigraph: William Shakespeare, *Hamlet*, act 3, scene 2, lines 1, 14–15, 18.

CHAPTER 7. TERRORIST ATTACK CYCLE

1. See William H. McRaven, *Spec Ops: Case Studies in Special Operations Warfare: Theory and Practice* (New York: Ballantine Books, 1996); John R. Boyd, "The Essence of Winning and Losing," a slide set/briefing, January 28, 1995.

2. See "Generic Terrorist Attack Timeline" slide, Sinai, "Red Teaming the Terrorist Threat," PowerPoint presentation.

3. This conclusion was derived from discussions with Matt Begert, a Mirror Image cell leader for the Terrorism Research Center for numerous courses throughout the United States in 2008 and 2009. Lieutenant Colonel Begert (USMC, ret.) has a Marine Corps special forces background and a university degree in anthropology, so he has the rare ability to approach and think deeply about red team training from both the terrorist and responding forces perspectives.

4. Robert J. Bunker and John P. Sullivan, *Suicide Bombings in Operation Iraqi Freedom*, Land Warfare Paper 46W (Arlington, Va.: Institute of Land Warfare, Association of the United States Army, September 2004).

5. McRaven, *Spec Ops,* 4.

6. Ibid., 4–6.

7. United Airlines Flights 175 and 93, respectively. See Matt Begert, "Principles of Special Ops" (El Segundo, Calif.: NLECTC–West, June 2004), PowerPoint presentation.

8. MOOSEMUSS stands for maneuver, objective, offense, simplicity, economy of force, mass, unity of command, surprise, and security. A good law enforcement special operations discussion of these nine tenets can be found in Charles "Sid" Heal, *Sound Doctrine: A Tactical Primer* (New York: Lantern Books, 2000), chapter 5, "Tactical Principles," 53–58.

9. See Alon Stivi, "On Location Responders: Progressive School Safety Measures," PowerPoint presentation (Costa Mesa, Calif.: DMI, Inc., March 2009).

10. See Robert J. Bunker, "Leadership and OPFOR Networks," in *Advancing Policing Leadership: Lessons Learned and Preferable Futures,* ed. Joseph A. Schaffer and Sandy Boyd, Futures Working Group 6 (Washington, D.C.: U.S. Department of Justice, March 2010), 122–37.

11. Malcolm N. Nance, *Terrorist Recognition Handbook,* 2nd ed. (New York: CRC Press, 2008).

12. The backpack used in the mall food court scenario contained books and other heavy objects. No simulated IED was used, as the local police and mall security had no idea that we were engaging in privately provided training. Bunker did not want to spend a night or more in jail attempting to clear up any misunderstandings in case his "nefarious activities" were discovered. They were not.

13. The statement is made by George C. Scott, playing the title role in the movie *Patton;* see "George S. Patton," Wikipedia.com, http://en.wikipedia.org/wiki/George_S._Patton.

14. Conversation in Hanoi, April 1975, quoted in Harry G. Summers, Jr., *On Strategy: A Critical Analysis of the Vietnam War* (Novato, Calif.: Presidio Press, 1982), 1.

CHAPTER 8. FUTURE TERRORISM

Epigraph: Statement by a hypothetical military analyst belonging to the military forces (BlackFor) of a criminal-state contained in a U.S. Army War College document.

1. A discussion of some of these concepts can be found in Sid Heal, "Tactical Concepts: Intelligence (Trends, Potentials, Capabilities and Intentions)," *Tactical Edge* (Winter 2000): 76–77.

2. "Futures Research," Police Futurists International (PFI) Web site, http://www.policefuturists.org.

3. See Robert J. Bunker, "Terrorists and Laser Use: An Emergent Threat," *Studies in Conflict and Terrorism* 31, no. 5 (May 2008): 434–55.

4. Collar bombs are IEDs placed around the necks of victims held for ransom (typically in Colombia); and internal body bombs are predicted to be utilized by suicide bombers against high-value targets such as VIPs and commercial aircraft; platter charges are IEDs that project metal platters (such as manhole covers) at targets; and thermobaric explosives utilize fuel (vapor or particulate matter) suspended in air, which, when detonated, creates intense overpressure effects.

5. Staff attorneys, IBLS Editorial Board, "Internet Law—Internet Hunting in the U.S.A.," Internet Business Law Services Web site, http://www.ibls.com.

6. Sylvia Moreno, "Mouse Click Brings Home Thrill of the Hunt: Critics Move to Stop Tex. Online Business," *Washington Post*, Sunday, May 8, 2005, p. A01.

7. These initiatives have utilized commercial products such as RapidResponder by Prepared Response, Inc. (http://www.prepared response.com) and fourDscape by Balfour Technologies, LLC (http://www.bal4.com).

8. Netwar concepts were initially developed by John Arquilla and David Rondfelt in 1996. Since the emergence of these concepts, numerous other netwar writers have emerged. For a basic primer, see John Arquilla and David Rondfelt, eds., *Networks and Netwars* (Santa Monica, Calif.: RAND, 2001).

9. Ibid., ix.

10. "Hizballah/Hizbollah/Hizbullah/Hezbollah," http://www.Globalsecurity.org.

11. See the five-part series "Professors in the Trenches: Deployed Soldiers and Social Science Academics," *Small Wars Journal* (April 2009), http://www.smallwarsjournal.com.

APPENDIX 2. HOSTAGE-TAKING AND ACTIVE-AGGRESSOR SIMULATIONS

1. Brian Jenkins, *International Terrorism: A New Mode of Conflict*, California Seminar on Arms Control and Foreign Policy Research Paper 48 (Los Angeles: Crescent Publication, 1975), 4.

2. This guidance for contact, and entry if necessary to do so, varies slightly from precepts coming from the National Tactical Officers Association (NTOA) and now utilized by the Advanced Training Unit of the Seattle Police Department. This form of tactical decision making focuses on the question, Is direct and immediate intervention (entry) *necessary* and *likely to save lives?* Until this form of rapid intervention training becomes more widespread and is accepted by the majority of police departments and law enforcement agencies, contact (and entry if necessary) will remain the preferred procedure to respond to these incidents. The above information was provided by, and much of this appendix concerning tactical decision making and incident response has benefited from, extensive group discussions on the pfimembers@ yahoo.groups (Police Futurists International) group server during the week of April 20, 2009. Special thanks to John A. Jackson and T. Joseph Fountain for their especially valuable comments and observations.

Selected Bibliography

Anderson, Sean K., with Stephen Sloan. *Historical Dictionary of Terrorism.* 3rd ed. Lanham, Md.: Scarecrow Press, 2009.

Bloom, Mia. *Dying to Kill: The Allure of Suicide Terror.* New York: Columbia University Press, 2005.

Bunker, Robert J. *Red Teaming.* Subject bibliography. Quantico, Va.: FBI Library, December 2008.

Coram, Robert. *Boyd: The Fighter Pilot Who Changed the Art of War.* New York: Back Bay Books, 2004.

Culpepper, Anna M. *Effectiveness of Using Red-Teams to Identify Maritime Security Vulnerabilities to Terrorist Attack.* Monterey, Calif.: Naval Postgraduate School, September 2004.

Dobson, Christopher, and Ronald Payne. *Terrorists: Their Weapons, Leaders and Tactics.* New York: Facts on File, 1982.

Forest, James J., ed. *Countering Terrorism and Insurgency in the 21st Century.* 3 vols. Westport, Conn.: Praeger, 2007.

Giduck, John. *Terror at Beslan.* Golden, Colo.: Archangel Group, 2005.

Gold, Ted, and Bob Hermann. *Defense Science Board Task Force on the Role and Status of DoD Red Teaming Activities.* Washington, D.C.: Office of the Under Secretary of Defense for Acquisition, Technology, and Logistics, September 2003.

Grossman, Dave. *On Combat.* Belleville, Ill.: PPCT Research Publications, 2004.

Gunaratna, Rohan. *Inside Al Qaeda: Global Network of Terror.* London: Hurst, 2002.

Hawley, Chris, Gregory G. Noll, and Michael S. Hildebrand. *Special Operations for Terrorism and HAZMAT Crimes*. Chester, Md.: Red Hat Publishing, 2002.

Heal, Charles "Sid." *Sound Doctrine: A Tactical Primer*. New York: Lantern Books, 2000.

Hoffman, Bruce. *Inside Terrorism*. London: Victor Gollancz, 1998.

Jenkins, Brian. *New Modes of Conflict*. Santa Monica, Calif.: RAND, 1983.

Johnson, Rob. "The Question of Foreign Cultures: Combating Ethnocentrism in Intelligence Analysis (Case Study Two: The Red Team)," chapter 6 in Johnson, *Analytic Culture in the US Intelligence Community*. Washington, D.C.: Center for the Study of Intelligence, Central Intelligence Agency, 2005.

Katona, Peter, Michael D. Intriligator, and John P. Sullivan, eds. *Countering Terrorism and WMD*. London: Routledge, 2006.

Katz, Samuel M. *Jihad in Brooklyn: The NYPD Raid That Stopped America's First Suicide Bombers*. New York: New American Library, 2005.

Longbine, David F. *Red Teaming: Past and Present*. Fort Leavenworth, Kans.: School of Advanced Military Studies, United States Command and General Staff College, 2008.

Lynch, Michael D. "Developing a Scenario-Based Training Program." *FBI Law Enforcement Bulletin* 74, no. 10 (October 2005): 1–8.

Malone, Timothy G., and Reagan E. Schaupp. "The 'Red Team': Forging a Well-Conceived Contingency Plan." *Aerospace Power Journal* 16, no. 2 (Summer 2002): 22–33.

Marcinko, Richard. *Red Cell: The True Story*. Brentwood, Calif.: L.O.T.I. Group Productions, 1994. VHS, color, 55 minutes.

McRaven, William H. *Spec Ops: Case Studies in Special Operations Warfare: Theory and Practice*. Novato, Calif.: Presidio Press, 1995.

Moore, Judy, John Whitely, and Rick Craft. *Red Gaming in Support of the War on Terrorism: Sandia Red Game Report*. Albuquerque, N.Mex.: Sandia National Laboratories, February 2004.

Murphy, Paul. *The Wolves of Islam: Russia and the Face of Chechen Terror*. Washington, D.C.: Brassey's, 2004.

Nance, Malcolm. *Terrorist Recognition Handbook: A Practitioner's Manual for Predicting and Identifying Terrorist Activities*. London: Taylor and Francis, 2008.

O'Neill, Bard E. *Insurgency and Terrorism: From Revolution to Apocalypse*. 2nd ed., rev. Washington, D.C.: Potomac Books, 2005.

Osborn, Jon. "Single officer response to active shooters." *Tactical Edge* 28, no. 2. (Spring 2010): 38–44.

Pasquarett, Michael. *Wargaming Homeland Security to Meet the Challenges Confronting 21st Century America.* Issues Paper 03-02. Carlisle Barracks, Penn.: Center for Strategic Leadership, U.S. Army War College, 2002.

Poole, H. John. *Militant Tricks: Battlefield Ruses of the Islamic Insurgent.* Emerald Island, N.C.: Posterity Press, 2005.

———. *Tactics of the Crescent Moon: Militant Muslim Combat Methods.* Emerald Island, N.C.: Posterity Press, 2004.

Red Team Journal. http://redteamjournal.com.

Sageman, Marc. *Leaderless Jihad: Terror Networks in the Twenty-First Century.* Philadelphia: University of Pennsylvania Press, 2008.

———. *Understanding Terror Networks.* Philadelphia: University of Pennsylvania Press, 2004.

Sandoz, John F. *Red Teaming: A Means to Military Transformation.* Alexandria, Va.: Institute of Defense Analysis, Joint Advanced Warfighting Program, January 2001.

Sinai, Joshua. "Red Teaming the Terrorist Threat to Preempt the Next Waves of Catastrophic Terrorism." Arlington, Va.: ANSER, 2003. PowerPoint presentation at the 14th Annual NDIA SO/LIC Symposium and Exhibition, February 12, 2003.

Sloan, Stephen. *Simulating Terrorism.* Norman: University of Oklahoma Press, 1981.

———. *Terrorism: The Present Threat in Context.* Oxford: Berg, 2006.

Springer, Devin R., James L. Regens, and David N. Edger. *Islamic Radicalism and Global Jihad.* Washington, D.C.: Georgetown University Press, 2009.

Sullivan, John P., and Alain Bauer, eds. *Terrorism Early Warning: 10 Years of Achievement in Fighting Terrorism and Crime.* Los Angeles: Los Angeles County Sheriff's Department, 2008.

Sullivan, John P., Robert J. Bunker, Ernest J. Lorelli, Howard Seguine, and Matt Begert. *Jane's Unconventional Weapons Response Handbook.* Alexandria, Va.: Jane's Information Group, 2002.

Tactical Decision Games (TDG) Series. *Marine Corps Gazette.*

Tactical Edge, The. The magazine of the National Tactical Officers Association (NTOA).

University of Foreign Military and Cultural Studies (UFMCS). *Red Team Leader's Course Topical Bibliography.* Fort Leavenworth, Kans.: UFMCS, January 24, 2007.

INDEX

FIELD NOTES

FIELD NOTES

FIELD NOTES